CASE CLOSED

Top Secrets from Former McKinsey Consultants & Interviewers to Landing Consulting Job Offers

Sean Huang

* * *

Case Closed is an award-winning, detailed guide to acing the consulting interview. Other consulting prep materials are written by those who have been out of the industry for decades. Case Closed is the only guide written by former McKinsey consultants and interviewers who have been intimately involved in the interview process in the last 2 years.

This authoritative resource covers some never-covered-before topics, including:

1) How to write your resume to attract the attention of resume-graders and recruiters at McKinsey, Bain, and BCG

2) Why the "personal experience" (fit) interview matters, what interviewers are probing for, and what types of experiences to prep

3) How the interviewers evaluate your case performance: what matters, and what doesn't

4) How to tackle non-traditional cases that interviewers may throw at you, which no canned framework from the typical case interview books can help with

5) How to prep if you have 60 days, 30 days, or just 2 weeks before your expected first interview
6) How to hack both in-person interactions and video interview interactions, in a time of COVID-19

7) The surprisingly good — and surprisingly bad — questions to ask your interviewer during Q&A

8) How to master innovative, universally-adaptable case interview frameworks. Any candidate can regurgitate the frameworks from Case In Point or Case Interview Secrets; nothing there will "wow" an interviewer

9) Countless example cases spanning profitability, new market entry, new product / growth, pricing, M&A, and even non-traditional archetypes

Whether you are a current undergrad or MBA looking for an internship or full-time role, or an experienced professional, Case Closed is an investment into your professional future. Stand out from the pack with the latest, cutting-edge secrets to wow your consulting case interviewers.

Sean Huang's former proteges span undergraduates, MBAs, advanced degree holders, and experienced hires. These students have landed job offers at top consulting firms, including McKinsey, BCG, and Bain; many have also used the structured thinking he has taught them to land roles at Goldman Sachs IBD, Google BizOps & Strategy, as well as at Fortune 500 strategy groups.

"Case Closed has been a lifesaver. It truly contains everything you need to know to ace your consulting interviews and Sean explains things in a clear manner that is easy to understand. After studying Case Closed, I landed my dream job at McKinsey and I've raved about this book to all my friends."
—McKinsey New York full time offer, Wharton MBA

"I used to be intimidated by the notorious consulting case interviews. For anyone looking to get a job offer to a top consulting firm, Case Closed is honestly the best interview prep book (and I've read all of them). The case interviews in Case Closed were by far the best and

most similar to the cases I got in the actual interviews."
—Bain San Francisco internship offer, UC Berkeley Haas (under-graduate)

"In my panic, I read all of the case interview frameworks from different case prep books. And that ended up confusing me more because there were so many frameworks but no easy way to remember when to use what. Case Closed walks you through the interview process in such a great way that I started loving case interviews and landed the job."
—BCG Boston full time offer, University of Virginia (under-graduate)

CONTENTS

"Pls fix asap, thx"

- ANONYMOUS CONSULTANT

INTRODUCTION

I n 2001, a horrific and tragic event hit New York City, and shocked the world. Ask anyone on the streets and they should know about the terrorist attack on 9/11 that killed 2,977 people and struck the Twin Towers at the World Trade Center and the Pentagon in Washington D.C. Five years later, construction of the 9/11 memorial and museum began. In 2014, the doors of the 9/11 memorial and museum opened to the public. Since then, more than four million people have visited the site. The soaring skyscraping towers and wide but deep ingenious waterfall construction mark the site, where visitors marvel the architectural prowess and reflect on the stories of that monumental event. The 9/11 memorial and museum has become one of the most notable tourist attractions in New York City. Yet very few people know that a small team of consultants from one of the top consulting firms was the brain behind designing, planning, and overseeing this massive project.

Think about all the businesses, organizations, and products you interact with in your daily life. The breakfast cereals that you loved as a kid, the yogurt that you grab on the way to work, the bank which issued your credit card, and many more. Or perhaps you read the news recently that the Pope was visiting your city or that your country's Ministry of Health is planning on rolling out a new vaccine program. Chances are, there have been consultants at work helping to strategize, optimize, and create the product or event that you are experiencing.

There are many types of consulting. This book will focus on management consulting, which is the type of consulting that some of the most well-known consulting firms, such as McKinsey, Bain, and the Boston Consulting Group, provide. The very nature of consulting is to use your brains and skills to solve problems, ultimately delivering lasting value and impact to clients. These problems can be categorized in a matrix where along one axis, you have function - marketing and sales, strategy, operations, risk management - and along the other axis, you have industry - healthcare, financial services, retail, pharmaceuticals and medical products, and more. A consulting project might look like helping a large healthcare system develop its five-year growth strategy or helping a breakfast-food focused multinational corporation develop an innovation department to create a new and healthy snack.

What makes consulting alluring as a career option is both the variety of exciting, high-impact work, and the diversity of clients from different industries. If you love problem solving, creative thinking, traveling to new places constantly, and embarking on a challenging and rewarding career, this could be a career that fits your calling. It could be for you.

The first step to joining a consulting firm is the interview process. This book will walk you through the key things you need to know to prepare and perform well in the interviews. We will teach you what consulting firms are looking for in a future employee, go through the resume preparation, and equip you with the necessary tools to ace the case interview.

As a former consultant in McKinsey's New York Office until recently, I have seen all the ins-and-outs of the interview process and felt like the most commonly used case interview prep books are no longer relevant with today's interview style and frameworks. During my time at McKinsey, I have reviewed and scored thousands of resumes, done countless case interview preps, and interviewed so many hopeful candidates. I developed the Case Closed system to drastically simplify the case interview prep process for candidates and ensure that they have a good grasp on the truly key concepts needed.

Whether you are currently an undergraduate or business school student hoping to intern at a top-tier firm, or an experienced professional looking to lateral in, if you are interested in landing a consulting job, this book is for you!

RESUME

In October 2020, Business Insider reported that the odds of getting hired by McKinsey & Company are less than 1%. According to the article, McKinsey received 800,000 applications in 2018 but only 8,000 people that year received offers. If you look at these odds, you are likely to be disheartened. However, your chances of success are not dictated by sheer odds -- what such news reports do not tell you is there is a formula to acing the interview process. We will go through the key things you need to do to stand out in the interview process and secure an offer. This chapter will walk you through the first step of the interview process, which is developing and submitting your resume.

Every single interview process will start with a resume. The resume is a way for you to tell your story, your experiences, and strengths in one-page (more is not better, and the best resumes are one-page long). While screening resumes, consulting firms look out for four distinct areas. Each of these areas are critical to success in consulting work. Consulting firms are looking for candidates who can demonstrate a high aptitude in those areas that indicate someone who will be a distinctive team member and consultant.

These four key areas are:

- Problem solving

- Achievement or entrepreneurship

- Personal impact

- Leadership

Problem solving is the basis of any consulting engagement. Consultants are hired to help clients solve difficult problems in their businesses, develop appropriate solutions, and implement these solutions. As a result, this job requires not only strong intellectual thinking, creativity and flexibility in problem solving, but also a logical, practical sense of what could work and the ability to understand the nuance of driving large-scale change in a big organization.

Achievement or entrepreneurship is a leading indicator for a candidate who will be a high performer in the future as well. If you have been able to achieve great results during your time as a student or previous career roles, the likelihood that you would be able to achieve similarly great results in a consulting role is therefore perceived to be much higher. Consulting firms, and companies in general, believe that to achieve success in your prior pursuits, you must have been able to juggle multiple stakeholders and deadlines, pursue your goals with passion, determination, and a lot of hard work. Consulting firms prize these traits as they are crucial to delivering a distinctive client experience.

Personal impact refers to the interpersonal or relational impact that you have had on other people in your experiences. As a consultant, you will need to work very closely with a wide range of individuals on a day-to-day basis. These people could be your clients, team members, other colleagues in the same company who support your work on analytics, design, etc., or even people from third-party organizations who help with one or another input for your team's work. Driving a consulting engagement to successful completion *always* requires the involvement and support of other individuals. As such, consulting firms keep a keen eye out for how you have personally impacted the lives of other people in your experiences.

Leadership is the last key trait that consulting firms look for in your resume, and interview. Consultants need outstanding leadership skills to drive positive change in large and often very complex organizations. As a consultant, you will need to lead teams, drive your workstreams forward, and influence clients to implement the changes that you are proposing. Leading people in the direction that you think is best and fostering good team environments are integral to success in consulting.

Your resume should demonstrate all four of these key areas. Consulting firms look for candidates who are well rounded individuals, who have a good mix of these skills, and who are fun to work with.

Practical Writing Tips For Developing Your Resume

When developing your resumes, use these practical tips to really highlight your strengths.

(1) Include numerical impact where possible. Consulting firms interpret your "achievement" and "personal impact" through these numbers. How many people were in your group or club or event that you impacted? What was the financial or user volume or cost impact from your work? Why would you consider this work that you are describing to be a top achievement?

E.g., "Improved click-through rate with new advertising placements with Growth Marketing team" should be "Improved click-through rate by 230% with new advertising placements which drove an additional $800K in revenue over 3 months through cross-functional work with Growth Marketing team"

E.g., "VP of Finance in SingingCats a capella group" should be "VP of Finance in 50-member SingingCats a capella group, managing annual budget of > $10,000"

E.g., "Trained new sales and customer success teammates on product updates" should be "Trained 35 new sales and customer success teammates on 100+ product updates"

Some examples of numerical impact are "XX people/member/audience", "XX% y-o-y or m-o-m increase", "XX ROI", "XX% growth", "$XXM or $XXK revenue or cost impact".

(2) Use high-impact action-oriented words when describing your experiences. These action words help to signal to the consulting firm that you were the one driving these results. How did you lead this project or participate in a way that demonstrated your skills? How did you solve the problem you were faced with?

E.g., "Did customer demos and weekly product updates for clients like Google" should be "Created and owned end-to-end development of 3 customer demos and set up structure for detailed weekly product updates for clients like Google"

E.g., "Owner of P&L for $50M Electronic category on Amazon.com" should be "Owned and actively managed P&L for $50M Electronic category on Amazon.com by engaging supplies, negotiating costs, setting prices, and managing assortment"

Some examples of high-impact action-oriented words are "strategized", "quarterbacked", "oversaw", "launched", "created", "developed", "delivered", "trained", "ran", "constructed", "built", "managed", "identified", "led", "closed", "achieved", "conducted", "programmed", etc.

(3) Quantify the extent of your impact over time. How long did it take for you to create this product? How long did it take for you and your company to see the results you mentioned? Adding a time bound to your experiences helps to demonstrate your achievement and impact even more.

E.g., "Launched three digital marketing campaigns with suppliers, resulting in 200% increased revenue in six months"

E.g., "Achieved $120M of supply chain savings in two years and grew profitability of three critical community hospitals by 3.5x in 8 months"

Some examples of time periods are "by X months or years", "in X quarters", "for X holiday", "for X monthly or weekly meetings".

(4) Sell the entrepreneurial aspect of your work where possible. Was this the first time this strategy has been done before or were you the person who created it? Did you have to do everything from scratch?

E.g., "Project built new digital consumer product from non-existent to 5+ million customers and $50B in revenue in 2 years"

E.g., "Developed >30 marketing campaign pilots to test over 3-month period to increase efficiency of $10M yearly spend on paid search marketing (Google AdWords, FB Ads)"

(5) Write your resume as though your reviewer is a 12-year-old child. Do not assume that your reviewer knows what a "Business Development Lead" is or what a "Category Specialist" does. The terminology in your resume should make sense and be understandable to your reviewer. Avoid abbreviations where

possible. If you are part of a club with an uncommon name, explain in a few words what the club is. There is no hard and fast rule for this - just try to put yourself in the reviewers' shoes and ask yourself if you would know or understand what that phrase in your resume means.

E.g., "VP of Finance in SingingCats" should be "VP of Finance in 50-member SingingCats, a capella group"

E.g., "President of Columbia MEDLIFE Chapter" should be "President of Columbia MEDLIFE Chapter, a non-profit medical volunteer club"

E.g., If you worked at "BarkBox", you could write "BarkBox (Series X box-subscription startup for dog owners)"

Structure Of Your Resume

(1) Structure your resume based on most important and relevant to least important and relevant. If you are currently an undergraduate student, your resume should start with education on the top, followed by internship experiences, and then additional information, such as skills, interests, languages, etc. at the bottom. If you are currently a working professional, your resume should start with working experiences at the top, followed by education, and then additional information. If you are in an MBA or graduate school program, your resume could take either format - either work or education at the top, followed by the remaining categories.

(2) Do not create a laundry list of all your experiences. Your reviewers care about what is most important and most recent.

(3) In the education section, it is not recommended for you to list all your education experiences (limit this to two educational experiences). If you are in a graduate program, you will

likely list your graduate program and undergraduate program.

(4) In the work experiences section, list the top 2-4 work experiences depending on how recent and impactful they were. If you had worked at your last two companies for a total of 10 years, you should list those two experiences. If you have worked at 4 companies for the last 5 years, you should list all those roles. The rule of thumb is to list the maximum of either 4 work experiences or work experiences that are within the last 10 years.

(5) Include relevant educational scores as appropriate in your education section. Again, you want to use discretion when deciding whether to include these or not and make sure that they position you in the best light and do not detract from your other positive qualities. A bad educational score could raise a red flag to your reviewer before they have a chance to evaluate your other achievements. Note that if you are applying as an undergraduate to an internship or full-time role, you may be required to disclose GPA and SAT / ACT as part of your application.

GPA: If you are listing your graduate or undergraduate education, you should list your GPA unless you have a dismal score (a rule of thumb here would be if your GPA corresponded to a B- in your school)

SAT or ACT: If your most applicable standardized testing score was your SAT or ACT score that you took in high school and you are less than 5 years out of college, that is a good metric to include in your education under your undergraduate experience. If you were, or are, a humanities major in undergraduate, and achieved a good math score, you should also list the breakdown of your math and reading scores. You want to demonstrate to your reviewer that you are a well-rounded candidate who can think analytical and handle business-related math as well.

GMAT or GRE: If you have taken the GMAT or GRE exam and received a good score, you should list these scores in your resume instead of your SAT or ACT score.

(6) Prioritize the experiences in each section of your resume starting from most recent to least recent. For example, if you are currently in a graduate school program, your education section should have your graduate school information and your next most recent education program.

(7) Include any hobbies, extracurriculars, interests in the bottom additional information section. Consultants spend anywhere from 50 to 100 hours a week with each other in team rooms and it is vitally important that their colleague is someone who can have fun outside of work. Consultants joke about the "airplane test" -- would they want to spend hours on a plane, or in the airport, or in a car with you? Having interesting hobbies or, if you are lucky, an interest that catches the eye of your interviewer who might share that same interest as you, could be a great talking point in your interview. Have fun with this last section of your resume!

Does Networking Matter?

When recruiting season comes around, you have probably heard a great deal about networking. Consulting, however, is different from finance or law careers where networking is paramount to getting a job offer. Consulting firms determine first round interview candidates by an objective scoring system that they use across all resumes. Your resume is usually scored by two different individuals at the consulting firm, and ultimately bucketed into "clearly will be interviewed", "clearly WON'T be interviewed", and "borderline and needs to be discussed further". Only resumes with scores in the last category are discussed by the recruiting team to determine if they should pass to the next round or not. For these resumes which are on the "borderline", networking can give you a slight edge if you made a favorable impression on someone in the recruiting team (or the consultants involved in resume review) who can then speak up for you during the discussion. However, the individuals present at the networking event or workshop could not be the same people who are scoring your resumes. As such, go to networking events if you have the interest to do so, otherwise do not stress out about it.

INTERVIEW PROCESS

Once you have submitted your resume, you will wait weeks, sometimes months, for that email or phone call saying that you have an interview. You might obsessively check your email to see if anything came in or ask your friends every day if they have heard anything yet. Unfortunately, the waiting period while the consulting firm reviews your resume and the hundreds of thousands of other resumes that were submitted is part of the process. Instead of biting your nails and waiting anxiously for that first email inviting you to interview, use that time to turn your focus to prepping for the interview process.

This chapter will walk you through the classic interview process at the top consulting firms. Keep in mind that the aim of the interview process is two-fold:

- To enable the company to learn more about your skills and experience so that they can determine your suitability for a career at their company
- To allow you to learn more about what they do and who they are so that you can be clearer and more confident about your career choices

Interview Structure

Most consulting firm interview processes are structured as follows:

Initial phone interviews: One 30-minute interview, usually with an HR professional from the company. These interviews are usually "fit" interviews where the HR professional will ask you about your background, resume, and interest level. NOTE: *This may not be applicable for undergraduate candidates from "target" schools (i.e., where consulting firms recruit heavily from, such as certain Ivies).*

First-round interviews: Two 45-minute back-to-back interviews, usually with a junior-level or mid-level consultant. These interviews are usually carried out in-person on campus if you are at school, or in the closest local office, or over Zoom. These interviews will follow the structure of a typical consulting interview where a portion of each interview will cover "fit" and a portion will cover the "case".

Second-round or final-round interviews: Three 45-minute back-to-back interviews, usually with a senior-level (e.g., Partner) consultant. These interviews are usually carried out in-person at the office which you hope to receive an offer from. These interviews will follow the structure of a typical consulting interview where a portion of your interview will cover "fit" and a portion will cover the "case".

The Consulting Interview

Each interview you have with a consultant will follow a format of:

(1) Some sort of warm-up chat similar to breaking the ice at the start

(2) "Fit" or "Personal Experience Interview" questions

(3) Case interview questions

(4) Q&A session for you to ask your interviewer questions

Interview section	Approximate time	Overall score contribution
Warm-up chat	5 minutes	- Officially 0%, but influences first impressions and sociability perceptions
"Fit" or "Personal Experience Interview"	McKinsey: 15 to 20 minutes Bain & BCG: 10 to 15 minutes	- McKinsey scores this section as 50% - Bain & BCG as well as other consulting firms score this around 20%
Case interview	20 minutes	- McKinsey scores this section as 50% - Bain & BCG as well as other consulting firms score this around 80%
Q&A session	5 minutes	- Officially 0% but influences perception of "fit"

Keep in mind that each interview is fluid and interviewer dependent. The sequencing and time spent on each portion of the interview could differ greatly from interviewer to interviewer. One interviewer might choose to get through the case interview portion first and then dive into the "fit" portion. Another interviewer might spend no time at all on the warm-up chat, 5 minutes on the "fit" portion, and the remaining time on the cash interview because he or she cared more about the case interview than the other parts of the interview. Conversely, a different interviewer might spend 10 minutes on the warm-up chat, 15 minutes on the "fit", and 15 minutes on the case interview because they prioritize the behavioral fit.

Do not be surprised if the format of the interview changes and is not the same sequence you have practiced or experienced. When an interviewer moves from one section to the next, trust that the interviewer has already gotten the requisite information from that portion of the interviewer. Make sure you are alert and pay attention to these fluid transitions so that you do not risk answering questions inappropriately or without the right framework.

Thank You Emails

One question candidates often have is, "Should I send a thank-you email to my intervicwers after the interview?"

Truthfully, at the large consulting firms, it does not matter. The interviewer likely has a full slate of a day's interviews; at the end of the day, all the interviewers regroup with the recruiting team and share feedback. Most of the time, offers and rejections decisions are made during the discussion session. In other words, by the time your interviewer reads your thank you email, a decision has likely already been made. And in the case the interviewer *did* read your thank-you email, rest assured that it will not sway the decision either way. Conversely, if you didn't send a thank-you email, the interviewer will not be "dinging" you in her head for not sending one -- she has many other things on her full-time consulting project that she's worrying about instead.

That being said, the cost of sending a thank-you email is merely time. I would still suggest you write one. Remember to keep it simple and concise and try to reference one or two things that stood out during your interview (likely during the Q&A section). Even if it will not influence whether you get an offer, you never know when your path may cross with the interviewer again.

Video Interviews

Consulting video interviews are no different from other video interviews, and best practices also apply. In case you need a refresher on how to put your best foot forward in video interviews:

Good lighting. Ensure that the light source is in front of you (e.g., sitting in front of a window, or a lamp), and that there is no strong light source behind you.

Good video. Ensure that the camera is placed directly in front of you. In particular, if you are using an external monitor, but are using a laptop webcam, use only your laptop for the interview, so you are looking into the camera.

Good audio. Avoid relying on your computer's built-in speakers and/or microphones, and instead either wear earphones or a headset. This minimizes the chances of distracting echo or picking up too much background noise.

Test everything beforehand. If you know what platform will be used in advance (e.g., Zoom), ensure that you have the software installed, and you have tested your camera, microphone, and sound output.

Warm-Up Chat

Consultants interact heavily with people on a day-to-day basis.

They have mastered the art of "social talk" and getting to know someone. Many interviews will start with some warm-up chat. There is no hidden agenda here. Interviewers usually just genuinely want to know how you are doing and "break the ice" so to speak. This is your chance to make a good first impression. Walk confidently into the room, make eye contact, share a pleasant smile, and do a firm handshake. Sit down calmly and pretend that this is an acquaintance that you want to get to know better -- or better yet, be truly excited to get to know the interviewer better.

Some common warm-up questions will look like:

- How was your day so far?

- How are you doing?

- How was your flight here? How was your trip here?

- How do you like the office?

- Is this your first time in the city?

- Have you had breakfast yet?

Think of these questions as conversation starters that you might have with a friend or a date or coffee chat. Answer these questions politely and sincerely. For example, "I've had a great day so far. It is my first time in the city, and everything I've seen so far has been beautiful and historic." Another example could be "I haven't had breakfast yet, but I noticed some great brunch places around the office that I am excited to try later on."

Your interviewer might also ask you about something interesting that he or she had read on your resume. I had a friend who wrote that "fantasy football" was one of his interests in his resume. Coincidentally, he met an interviewer who also loved fantasy football and they spent the first 5 minutes of the interview just chatting happily about fantasy football, their teams, leagues, and more. This effectively broke the ice for them and helped my friend, and I imagine the interviewer as well, feel very at ease for the rest of the interview. I also had a friend who alluded to attending EDM concerts on her resume. Her Partner-level final round interviewer happened to also love EDM, and they ended up talking for 15 minutes on the favorite concerts that they have attended, and which artists were best live performers. Both friends received offers.

One note of caution that there is no need to overreact and add "extra" sass or spice. Trying to go for the extra funny or "smart" response could be potentially awkward. For example, "My day has been great. Of course, I'm excited to be in this office because I badly want to work here so nothing could really beat this day." Another example of a poor response could be, "I had really smooth travel to the city. I flew in early yesterday morning because I was worried about missing my flight or my flight being delayed. I then had an easy trip by train into the city from the airport. It was also simple to walk here from my hotel." This is oversharing and unnecessary, and risks coming across as awkward or overly nervous.

Most interviewers will ask you how you are doing. Answer them politely and sincerely and ask them a similar question back. Your interviewers will appreciate the thoughtfulness, and this will signal to them that you are not nervous.

Q&A Session

Every interview will usually end with 5 to 10 minutes at the end for you to ask your interviewer any questions. This is really your time to be the interviewer and ask thoughtful and provoking questions that will help you understand the job and company better. You should treasure this time as a window of opportunity to get an insight into where you are hoping to work.

You should prepare 5 to 7 questions before your interviews. These questions should be targeted questions that help you answer a question that you have about this career. Think about it this way: you are hoping to commit the next 2 years, potentially more, to this career and way of life. What is it truly like? Will you enjoy it? Is this a place you really want to spend almost 3,000 hours a year working in? What will life be after you leave this place?

Consulting is a great and rewarding career, but it is not perfect. No job is. However, consulting firms and recruiting companies will not often tell you these insights because they want and hope that you would join them. You need to do your due diligence. It is after all your life and your career.

Some potential questions that you could ask your interviewer:

(1) What do you wish you had known before working in consulting?

(2) What do you wish you had known about this company?

(3) If you could go back in time, what advice would you have wanted to give you younger self? (Note: this is a personal favorite of mine.)

(4) How long did you think you would work in consulting when you first joined? Has that changed and why?

(5) What do you want to do after consulting, and how will what you have learned on the job set you up for success?

(6) If you could, what is one thing you would change about the company?

(7) What is something you wish you could change about the role of consultants?

(8) Are you specialized in a function or industry? Why or why not?

(9) How do you think the role and the perception of consultants have changed over time?

(10) Tell me about a low point in your consulting career. Why was it tough?

(11) Why did you choose this consulting office?

(12) In your opinion, what are the best parts of being a consultant?

If you would like to take your question to the next level, try to work in something that the interviewer has already mentioned earlier in the interview, such as during the icebreaker or during the case. This shows that you were actively listening during the prior exchange, and you have cared enough to remember. For example, "You mentioned earlier that you've done a lot of work in the consumer-packaged goods space. That sounds awesome! Is this something that you've formally specialized in, and if so, how easy or hard was it to specialize?" However, note that if it appears forced, it will come across as awkward and may leave the interviewer with a bad taste in their mouth.

You should be creative and honest in your questions. Ask questions that are truly informative and additive to your knowledge base about the job and company. Refrain from asking "throw away" or "fluffy" questions unless the answer is truly interesting to you. Examples of such questions are:

What is your favorite consulting project? The reason why I would not advise asking this question is the answer to this rarely illuminates anything for the candidate. Does it matter what your interviewer's favorite project was? How does that impact what your consulting career could be like? A better question would be to ask, "What is your favorite consulting project and what were the defining qualities that made that project your favorite?" The second half of that question could be informative to a candidate.

What is your day-to-day like? This is a difficult question to answer and the most common response you will get is likely "every day is so different and no one day is the same". The truth is no one day is the same. A consultant's job consists of multiple different tasks and meetings, and no two days are exactly the same. You could be flying to a client site one day for a steering committee meeting, and the next day back in your home office for a lunch series with a Partner.

Steer away from questions that reveal your ignorance or lack of understanding about the company or role. Examples of such questions are:

- What type of consulting does the firm do?

- How many employees does the firm have?

- How big is the firm?

- How many offices does the firm have?

- What industries does the firm specialize in?

- How many consultants are hired each year?

- How often do you travel?

- When was the firm established?

- Where is the firm's headquarters?

These are questions that you can easily get the answers to by searching the company online and reading through the company's website or various forums. Before asking a question, ask yourself if the answer to this question is something unique that only your interviewer can provide. If the answer is yes, then go ahead and ask the question. If the answer is no, which means that multiple people can provide the exact same answer, then do not ask this question.

Finally, remember that you want to make sure you are making the right choice for you: while it may not sometimes feel that way, you are also interviewing the interviewer as well. Listen carefully to your interviewers' answers and try to glean as much wisdom as you can. Do you like what you hear? Or does what they say raise some yellow or red flags? Hopefully, their experiences can help to guide your career in the best direction for you.

BEHAVIORAL FIT INTERVIEW

Years ago, one of my friends told me this story about his interview. About 10 minutes into the "fit" portion of his summer internship interview with a Bain & Company partner, he knew he was not going to get an offer. This was his final round interview with a partner who would determine based on his answers to a couple of "fit" questions, whether he would integrate well with Bain culture and make a good consultant. He had thought the interview was going quite well. He had memorized a bunch of reasonable, nice answers about why he was interested in management consulting, why he thought he would be a good consultant, and why he thought Bain would be the best place to work. However, after 10 minutes of back-and-forth question and answer, he felt the partner mentally mark him with a large "X" and put him in the "reject" bucket. He could not quite understand why. He had these seemingly coherent answers "I love to travel and would make a great consultant", "I love working on exciting and challenging problems", "I enjoy working with clients", "I want to drive impact". Yet his intuition was right, and he did not get an offer.

Many candidates view the "fit" portion of the interview as the easy part compared to the case interview. However, this portion of the interview is often where candidates stumble because they fail to prepare. They think that this section should be easy to ace because the questions are all about them. I have heard many candidates say that they do not prepare for the "fit" interview because, of course, they should know themselves best and be able to answer these types of questions well.

While it is true that you are the most familiar with yourself, where these candidates stumble is often in their storytelling. Imagine yourself on a first date and your date asks, "I'm glad to finally meet you. Tell me about yourself". Do you start relating every fact about yourself starting from when and where you were born? Do you start with your high school years? Do you focus on your top achievement? What about the time when you were voted prom king? As you can see, there are a multitude of ways to answer a question about yourself, which makes it quite challenging to tell a compelling and memorable story.

Everyone has a different story. You need to think about how to best tell *your* story. The best guiding principle here is to weave a story with 1 to 3 overarching themes. Imagine that you are a newspaper journalist, what is the headline? Start with that headline and then go into detail around the story. Keep your story concise and focused on the most important things.

Interviewers remember stories and key achievements much better than they do a timeline of facts and results. I cannot count the number of times an interviewer has referred to a candidate by their achievement. "That Latin-dancing guy" or "the French-trained baker" or "the tennis captain" or "the photography guy" are some labels that interviewers might throw around. Even if you normally do not like being labeled, this is one of those times when being labeled as such and such helps you stand out amongst the sea of candidates. Interviewers can see between 6 to 12 candidates a day. What you want is to be remembered for a particularly memorable story such that at the end of the day, when your interviewers gather in a room to discuss who to move to the next round, your interviewer will see your name and pound on the table saying "Yes, this candidate should move to the next round. She demonstrated resilience and leadership in her tennis achievements."

Commonly Asked Fit Interview Questions

- Collective questions

  - Tell me about yourself

  - Walk me through your resume

  - Why consulting?

  - What do you think consultants do?

  - Why this consulting firm?

  - Why do you think we should hire you over others?

  - What are you looking for in your future job?

  - What are your flaws or weaknesses?

  - What are your strengths?

  - Where do you see yourself in 5 years? 10 years?

- Situational questions

  - Tell me of a time when you faced a moral dilemma

  - Tell me of a time when you had a conflict

  - Tell me of a time you showed leadership skills

- o Tell me of a time you were a team player

- o Tell me of a time when you started something new

- o Tell me of a time when you had to influence a group

- o Tell me of a recent crisis

- o Tell me of a time when you failed at something

- o Tell me of your greatest achievement

You can think of the behavioral or fit section of your interview in two categories. The first category of questions consists of collective or general behavioral questions. These are questions where two different candidates might provide a very similar answer. For example, if an interviewer were to ask, "Why consulting?" multiple candidates might give the same popular answer "You get to work and learn from highly intelligent and driven colleagues. You get to travel and work with different teams. The learning curve is steep and never ends."

The second category of questions consists of situational or, in terms of McKinsey speak, Personal Experience Interview (PEI) questions. These are questions where your answer should tell a story, and this should be a very personal story that only you can tell. This characteristic marks this category of questions very differently from the general behavioral questions. No two candidates can, or should, provide a similar answer because their experiences are different. Your interviewers will be trained to examine your past accomplishments and experiences in depth in order to determine if your skills and qualities would position you well for a successful career in consulting. As such, you need to be prepared to discuss your stories in a detailed way, focusing on your specific role, and describing your key actions and thoughts that were critical to success. This is especially the case for a McKinsey PEI interview where your interviewer will go deep on asking specific questions around your story. They might ask you any of the following probing questions:

- What did you do in that situation?

- What were you thinking?

- How did you react?

- What did you say to that person?

- What was the reaction of the group?

- Why did you do that?

- Why do you think the other person did that? What do you think he or she was thinking?

These are all questions that your interviewer is asking to gain a full picture of your experiences and your role in them. They want to get a look inside your brain and understand how you think, how you act, and, as a result, predict how you might think and act while on the job.

Preparing For Collective Or General Behavioral Questions

Refrain from regurgitating standard consulting answers. You have probably read dozens of "best" consulting answers. These might sound something like "you get to work as part of a team" or "you work on multiple projects" or "you will be exposed to multiple industries and functions" or "you are exposed to the top decision makers at large fortune 500 companies" or, one of the worst answers: "it is a prestigious job and you will have good chances of getting into business school". The fact is millions of other consulting hopefuls across the world have probably read these same answers. Your interviewers have probably heard these same reasons a thousand times over, and while spouting these same reasons will not likely ding your application significantly, it will not help to boost your chances.

Try to link your answers back to something personal. Ask yourself honestly about why you want the job and why you are excited about this company. Dig deeper into your own unique reasons for why you enjoy something. For example, you might enjoy problem solving, but do you know why you enjoy it? Do you enjoy problem solving because you like the thrill of seeing results quickly or because you like just being right or because you like helping others to solve problems? Link your enjoyment of problem solving to something that is more uniquely you. So instead of saying "I enjoy problem solving", try providing something with more depth such as "I have always enjoyed problem solving because the principle of servant leadership is something that I value tremendously. I believe that one cannot lead without serving, and one cannot serve without understanding what needs serving or problem solving. To me, solving problems helps other people lead better lives and is a way of service that I care strongly about."

When asked if you have any weaknesses, say yes! Nobody is perfect and saying that you have no weaknesses will be a red flag to your interviewer. Talk about a real, honest, and meaningful weakness, something that you are working hard to improve on. Please steer away from sharing weaknesses which are "fluffy" ("I am too much of a perfectionist"), or you are not working on / are intrinsic and cannot be easily worked on ("I have a tendency to be very lazy"), or which might make an interviewer feel uncomfortable ("I have difficulty staying committed to a significant other").

Choosing Stories For Behavioral Questions

Review the key qualities which consulting firms looked for in your resume, that are described in the resume section. These will also be the same qualities that they look for in your fit interview. Make sure that your stories demonstrate these key qualities and paint you in the most favorable light. If a story shows leadership, but also shows that you were impatient or rash, that is not a good story to share.

Review the commonly asked fit questions above. For each question, write out your answers as though you were actually asked this question in an interview. Prepare bullet point answers -- do not write a script, or else you run the risk of sounding overly rehearsed.

Choose memorable stories that clearly and articulately describe an experience that answers at least two of the questions above and demonstrate the key qualities mentioned. You should choose an experience which you could apply to either "Tell me of a time when you faced a moral dilemma" and "Tell me of a time you showed leadership skills". For example, "When I was in the military, I served as the Captain for the Infantry unit. While I was away from camp, one of my men, who was also a good friend of mine, was found to have been AWOL and I was responsible for deciding whether to put him in military prison or not."

Prepare at least 3 stories for the first round of interviews, and 5 stories for the second round of interviews. Keep in mind that you should not share the same story with your interviewers because your interviewers will debrief your interview and it will be perceived as problematic if you only had one story. In the first round of interviews, you will need to share at least 2 different stories. In the second round of interviews, you will need to share at least 3 different stories. You can re-use stories that you had shared in the first round of interviews as the likelihood of overlap in interviewers between the rounds is very low.

Preparing Stories For Behavioral Questions

For each of your 3-5 stories that you have chosen, set aside an afternoon's worth of time to go deep into each of the stories. Given that you will be asked extremely in-depth questions of whatever story you share, in-depth preparation is required, especially if they occurred more than a few months ago.

Start by writing down:

o What the "context" and the "problem" was

o What the "complications" were, if any

o Who the "main characters" were

o What the resolution was

Then, continue to peel the onion. Jot down notes on:

(1) As detailed as you can remember, things that you said, and things other "main characters" said

(2) How the unfolding events made you feel, and how they made the other "main characters" feel. Why did they behave the way they did? McKinsey consultants subscribe to the 'iceberg' model -- while the things people say and do are observable (the top of the iceberg), the thoughts, feelings, fears, etc. beneath the surface are not observable. What was 'below the iceberg' for you and the other 'main characters'?

(3) How did you convince people to do a certain thing, or perform a certain way? Pick examples where you used multiple ways of doing so, ideally by discerning what was 'below the iceberg' of others. For example, "I had ascertained that my man-

ager was feeling insecure about his performance, which was why he was applying significant, unfair pressure on me during my summer internship. So as part of building a further solid foundation to our relationship, I made sure to tell him that when I had a skip-level meeting, I was effusive about his skills as a manager, and that his manager agreed and thought very highly of him."

Behavioral Body Language

There is a large body of psychology research that has demonstrated a clear relationship between the non-verbal interaction between the interviewer and interviewee, and the outcome of the interview. Researchers have found that an observer could predict whether or not the interviewee would be offered the job from watching just the first 15 seconds of the tape - the handshake, the "hello" and very little else. What happened in those few, brief moments was enough to determine the candidate's future.

What is known as "thin-slicing" has become a widely discussed topic. The theory is that we make a reasonably accurate assessment of a person from observing just a few seconds, or a "thin slice", of their behavior. Research shows that we are able to make up our minds about someone in a matter of seconds and purely from that person's body language. This might feel unfair to an interviewee. You might think that you have the full 45-minutes and the power of your words to convince your interviewer. However, psychological research has demonstrated the non-verbal cues that you send to your interviewer are as important, if not more important, than the verbal cues.

As you prepare for your consulting interview, make sure that you practice good body language with these tips:

Shake hands with your interviewer, smile slightly, maintain good eye contact, and say "hello". Nothing more is expected from you and do not fumble or be anxious.

Move in a calm manner. Starting from your walk into the interview room, do not rush, run, or saunter. When taking out your pen and paper or sitting down, you should move at a measured and collected pace.

Practice smoothing out your facial expression. If your face looks tense, stressed out, or anxious, your interviewer will easily pick up on that.

Do not hunch when you sit. Sit with your shoulders pulled back in a relaxed position, your back should be straight, keep your chin and eyes focused on your interviewer.

Verbal Hiccups

Verbal hiccups refer to any meaningless or useless sounds, words, or phrases that an interviewee uses during his or her speech. Examples of these verbal hiccups are:

- Um
- Ah
- Hmm
- Like
- You know
- Okay so
- Uh

- Well

Although these hiccups seem harmless, they hurt your interview through making you seem less sure, less credible, and less believable. These verbal hiccups are in fact a "mind crutch" that many people use in a few situations:

- They struggle communicating articulately

- They are nervous or anxious

- They are not sure and lack confidence

- They have not fully formed what they want to say

- They are lying

As you can see, none of these reasons for using a verbal hiccup are good reasons. When you stay away from using such sounds and words, your speech becomes more fluent and you sound more confident to others. Practice these tips for avoiding verbal hiccups:

(1) Practice pausing instead of using your typical verbal filler

(2) Write out your speech so that you know exactly what you will say next (though ensure that you do not sound "overly rehearsed")

(3) Use other more formal speech transitions such as "on the other hand", "moving on to", "in the next case", "what we ended up seeing was"

Lastly, it is likely that you are using verbal hiccups more than you realize, especially if you have not yet made a conscious effort to excise them from your vocabulary. As uncomfortable as it may be, record yourself during your practice case interviews, and note your usage of these hiccups. You may be surprised!

Take On The Mindset Of A Salesperson

Every interview process is essentially a sales pitch. The product you are trying to sell is yourself, and the customer you are trying to sell to is the consulting firm and interviewers. Your resume is the marketing campaign with exciting and bold claims that lure the customer in. "Pick me," it says. "This product will help your consulting firm grow and succeed through its stellar problem-solving and leadership skills." During the interview, you are the salesperson. Through the "fit" and case interview, you are pitching your analytical skills, intellect, and articulate abilities, and hoping that the consumer is won over by your pitch and buys the product.

Keep that in mind throughout the interview process. This is your chance to shine and market your skills and abilities. You have just a few chances to really make your pitch and win the hearts and minds of your customer so do not be shy and hold back.

Practice Makes Perfect

After preparing your bullet point answers and stories, the last step here is to practice, practice, practice. This cannot be stressed enough. Practice delivering your lines smoothly and sincerely. You can practice in a few ways:

- Delivering your story while looking at a mirror

- Recording yourself and then reviewing the video

- Asking a friend or family member to ask you the

"fit" question to simulate a real interview

There are 3 distinct phases of well-executed fit interview practice:

Beginning - you have practiced very little, and you stumble over the delivery of your answers. There are probably a few verbal hiccups and filler words, as well as rough patches.

Middle - you have practiced a fair amount, to the point that you know the stories well -- perhaps too well. You can rattle off what the problem is, who the main characters are, and what the complications are, but it has gotten to the point that it sounds canned; rehearsed. This is where most people stop during interview prep, but DO NOT stop here.

End - Not only do you have your stories down cold, but you have also engineered the thoughtful pauses, hand gestures, smiles, etc. to the point where the retelling of the story feels completely natural. Think of yourself as an experienced Broadway actor or actress playing a role for the stage. Every night, when the curtains go up, they are able to show the same emotions -- and evoke in the audience the same emotions -- night after night. For firms like McKinsey, where fit interviews account for 50% of your interview score, you need to spend just as much time honing your fit interview as your case interview.

You might bemoan the work that needs to go into interview preparation, and truth to be told, interview preparation *is* a lot of work. However, if you truly want that consulting job offer, then you need to be willing to put in the work to get it.

The Airplane Test

The "fit" portion of the interview is also a way for an interviewer to judge your character and personality. Your interviewer is assessing whether you are someone he or she would want to spend anywhere from 40 to 60 hours a week together in a team room. Consultants work in tight knit teams of usually 2 to 6 people. They are often given a "team room" at the client site or in their offices (sometimes no larger than a janitor's closet), where most of the problem solving, deck making, and Excel modeling occurs.

You will often hear about "the airplane test", which is essentially the interviewer assessing whether you are someone he or she would want to spend an airplane ride with (or being stuck at the airport, thanks to flight delays!):

- Are you someone they can get along during a flight?

- Are you arrogant?

- Are you easy to talk to?

- Do you have a sense of humor?

- Are you an interesting person?

Although it is less common than you think to be on the exact same flight as your team members, this airplane test has become the standard behavioral threshold to determine if a candidate is someone you would want on your team from a personality standpoint. It is natural to want to work with someone who we can get along with and who is easy to like and talk to. No one likes working with a jerk, especially clients.

THE CASE
INTERVIEW

W hen even considering a career in consulting, you have probably already heard of the "case interview", which is a common source of dread for almost all consulting candidates. What is a case interview? Consulting firms believe the best way they can assess your problem solving skills is to discuss a typical consulting business problem with you - they call this a case study.

Case interviews are used as an interview tool to assess a candidate's problem solving skills. The case studies that you discuss during your interview reflect the typical problem solving challenges faced by consultants. During this discussion, your interviewer will assess many things, including:

(1) How you go about structuring an ambiguous business problem

(2) How you prioritize which issues are important in addressing the problem

(3) How you digest and process data

(4) How you develop reasonable conclusions and recommenda-

tions to solve the problem

(5) How you synthesize and articulate your findings

Regardless of what you have heard about case interviews, try them for yourself before making a judgment on them. In actuality, practicing case interviews is a great way to determine if you will enjoy consulting. If you enjoy dissecting the business problems in case interviews, the likelihood that you will enjoy consulting work is high because case interviews reflect what real consulting life is like. The converse is also true - if you do not enjoy case interviews, then you should think twice about whether you really want to pursue a consulting career.

Think Like A Business Owner

A simple trick to coming up with the most important issues to address a problem and the best recommendations to solve a problem is to think like a business owner. If you were the CEO of this company, what would you do? This is a mindset that will effectively help you hone in on real areas to go tackle versus regurgitate case frameworks that you have memorized. Approaching every single case interview as though you were truly the business owner helps to strip away unnecessary answers. You end up caring about the real issues that could impact your business and not some standard consulting answer you read about.

There Is No One Right Answer

Case studies are broad, two-way discussions, rather than one-way tests. There is no one perfect answer. Rather, you will be assessed more on how you go about dealing with the problem. Can you focus on the right issues? Can you think outside the box?

Can you think creatively in ways that will solve this problem? Your case interview will test many qualities about you, including:

- Flexibility

- Thinking fast on your feet

- Creativity

- Logic and reason

- Analytical ability

- Good listening

- Structured thinking

Your answers need to adapt to whatever case study your interviewer gives you, and your interviewer might not give you a "standard" case study as well; this is especially prevalent in final round interviews with Partner-level interviewers. For example, one interviewer gave a case where a client's private jet lease was expiring in two weeks and they wanted your thoughts on whether they should rent a corporate airplane or maintain their private jet. Another interviewer, who lived and worked in Washington D.C., gave a case where the business owner of a food truck she frequented was wondering if he should close down the business and go back to school or whether he should continue running the food truck. These are not conventional case studies, but that does not mean that you should panic. The same problem solving skills should apply in these case interviews as well.

The Case Interview Format

The case interview format is, in truth, initially quite awkward. There is a certain structure and style to it that is not natural. However, you can learn this style quite quickly through preparation and practice. A typical case interview usually takes the following format:

- Interviewer: Imagine you have a client, ABCDE, who has experienced declining profits in the past five years...

- Candidate: [furiously jots down notes on the case study problem]

- Interviewer: [provides rest of the case study problem and stops]

- Candidate: Great, can I ask you a couple of clarifying questions?

- Interviewer: Yes, go ahead

- Candidate: [asks a clarifying question] You mentioned that the client had XXX, is that correct?

- Interviewer: Yes

- Candidate: [asks a probing question] Is there any additional information about the client's YYY?

- Interviewer: No

- Candidate: Okay great, thank you

- Interviewer: [asks the first case question] What do you think are the main drivers behind this client's declining profitability?

- Candidate: [asks for some time, usually 30 to 120 seconds]

Can I take a few moments to lay out my thoughts?

- Interviewer: Yes, go ahead

- [90 seconds later...]

- Candidate: [provides structure to answer the first question] I believe there are five potential drivers behind this. First, AAA. Second, BBB. Third, CCC., Fourth, DDD. And fifth, EEE.

- Interviewer: [moves on to second question] Great, what about...?

- Candidate: [asks for some time again] Let me take some time to jot down some thoughts

- [60 seconds later...]

- Candidate: [provides structured answer to second question]

- Interviewer: [moves on to third question] Assuming that XXX has been declining in recent years, what could you explore to reverse this trend?

- Candidate: [asks for some time again] Let me take some time to jot down some thoughts

- [60 seconds later...]

- Candidate: [provides structured answer to third question]

- [Case continues till all questions are asked and answered]

What did you notice about this case interview format? From this case interview format, there are three main stylistic points that you should note and practice:

- Do not be afraid to ask clarifying questions. Information is critical to helping anyone make good business decisions. Make sure that you are in possession of all the necessary information around this business problem, but do not go overboard or overly pedantic with small nuances or details that are not relevant to the case.

  - "Great, can I ask you a couple of clarifying questions?"

  - "You mentioned XXX, is that correct?"

  - "You said that the objective is to reduce costs. Is that correct? Are there any other objectives?"

- Take some time to pause and think at each question and answer juncture. One of the fatal flaws that candidates make is they hear a question, think of a rapid response, and fire off the first three thoughts that come to mind. This ends up resulting in a poor response as the candidate likely has not thought the question through, nor developed a structure and coherent reply, nor delivered his or her response in a measured and well-organized way. A good rule of thumb is to always take some time to pause and think through your response before speaking. You can take up to 2 minutes to gather your thoughts comfortably. In fact, interviewers prefer if you take some time to think through your response before spit balling the first thoughts off the top of your head. One thing to note is after the first ask for time, you do not need to consistently ask again. You can just state politely that you are going to take some time to think about your response.

  - "Can I take a few moments to lay out my thoughts?"

  - "Let me take some time to jot down some thoughts"

- Structure every single response that you provide. An easy way to structure responses is to provide clear, signposts to each bullet point in your answer. Given that the case interview is done verbally, you want to help your interviewer follow along with your thinking in simple ways.

  o Numbering: First, second, third, etc.

  o Transitional words: "The next area", "Lastly", etc.

The Case Interview Structure

You might have read that there are different types of case questions you could get. Market sizing questions, brainteaser, purely numerical questions, and business case questions, among others. However, this is no longer the case, and this is outdated information. The modern case interviews are rarely, if ever, just purely a market sizing question or a purely numerical question. Across the top consulting firms, case interviews usually follow this structure:

- Business case problem statement

- 1 overview-type question (e.g., what are the main drivers, what are the key areas to look at)

- 1 to 3 issue-analysis questions (e.g., what are potential reasons why ticket pricing has not changed, what methods could you employ to test whether there are strong revenue improvement opportunities with this marketing approach)

- At least 1 to 2 data-driven or math-related questions (e.g., sizing the market, determine the average cost of acquiring a new subscriber, determine the potential revenue from launching this product)

- Synthesis and recommendation

Data-Driven Or Math-Related Questions

Many candidates are intimidated by math-related questions. The idea of having to do calculations on the spot, just using pen and paper, tends to induce anxiety. Firstly, do not worry if you do not know the size of populations around the globe or the number of children under the age of 18 in the U.S. The main purpose of data-driven or math-related questions is to understand your thought process, *not* get to the most accurate mathematical answer. Secondly, these math questions are *designed to be solved in a few minutes using pen and paper*. They usually only involve basic mathematical calculations, such as addition, subtraction, multiplication, and division. Thirdly, where a piece of critical data is not available, you can and should make assumptions. Lastly, memorize a handful of key facts and numbers before your interview. These should be relevant numbers for your country or region. In the U.S., these are the key numbers you should memorize:

- U.S. population is 320 million (or 300 million, depending on which number is more convenient to use to make math cleaner)

- Life expectancy is generally 80 years and you can assume an even distribution between the different ages (i.e., 320 million people / 80 years = 4 million people per age year)

- Number of households in the U.S. is 100 million (implying average household size of 3 people per household)

When approaching any math-related question, here are the

steps you should follow, and remember to talk out loud your thought process:

- Step 1: What is this question asking you to solve? What is the final answer you are trying to get to?

  - Example: You need to calculate the change in revenue from three years ago to today)

- Step 2: What are the different data inputs you need to get to this final answer? Break down these data inputs into corresponding sub-data inputs till you have all the inputs you need. If a data input is not provided, you can ask your interviewer if that information is available, otherwise ask if you can make an assumption on what that number should be.

  - Example: Change in revenue from three years ago to today means you need the revenue from three years ago and the revenue today. Unless you already have the revenue numbers provided, you need to calculate these. To get revenue, you need the price multiplied by the quantity sold three years ago, and the same calculation today.

- Step 3: What is the easiest way of doing these calculations? Should you estimate or round off numbers to make the calculation easier?

  - Example: If you have 29.3 million, you can round this to 30 million so that it is easier to calculate.

Synthesis And Recommendations

Many case interviews will end with a synthesis-type question. Your interviewer might ask you, "Imagine if the CEO at our client were to walk into the room right now, what would you share with her about our team's findings?" The synthesis-type question is meant to test how concisely and eloquently you can summarize your case findings in a two-minute response. Some candidates might struggle with squeezing everything into two minutes, while some candidates might panic and say the first few things that pop into their head, without coherent structure.

The following approach works for all synthesis-type questions and will help you to ace these types of questions:

- During the course of your case interview, star, circle, or mark in some noticeable way to you the key points at each part of the case. This will help you to quickly identify the key points for your synthesis at the end of the case.

  - Example: If while doing a profitability case interview, you learn that high variable costs, particularly around raw materials, and decreasing volume of units sold were the two main drivers behind lower profits, you should draw a star next to those two points on your paper.

- When asked a synthesis-type question, structure your response using the hamburger analogy.

  - First, start with the bread. This would be your headline sentence that directly answers the business problem. For example, "The declining profits over the past three years was caused by higher raw material costs and lower volume of units sold."

  - Second, add your meat patty. This would be your substantiation for the headline sentence. For example, "Higher raw material costs were driven by both increased competition and climate changes which worsened crop yield."

o   Third, add your lettuce, cheese, and tomatoes.
This would be your recommendations for
how to fix the problem. For example, "Our
recommendations would be to look for lower
cost substitutions for these raw materials or
engage in renegotiations with the suppliers."

o   Lastly, add the other piece of bread to top your burger
off. This would be your suggested next steps, which
could be areas for further investigation to gain more
certainty or proposal to refine the recommendations
even more. For example, "We will need to investigate
reasons why there was increased competition for
the raw material to understand if the higher raw
material costs are temporary or long-term."

The Case Interview Assessment

A typical case interview can have as few as 3 questions to as
many as 5 to 7 case questions, which you can imagine as mini-
business problems within the larger case. Regardless of the
number of questions, your interviewer will be closely listening
to your answers and observing your thought process and communication during the interview to grade your performance.
Each consulting firm has their own interview grading rubric,
which differs slightly from one another. The general structure,
however, is that candidates need to make sure that they can
demonstrate all of these three skills competently:

- Critical reasoning skills: Structuring and logically
  and creatively responding to business questions

- Quantitative analysis skills: Understanding and
  performing simple math calculations on the spot

- Communication skills: Effectively synthesizing and providing a concise recommendation

If you messed up one area due to nervousness or a small mistake, such as a calculation error in the quantitative analysis section, but you were a strong performer in the other two areas, your interviewer might still choose to pass you on to the next round. So, if you happen to make a mistake during the interview, do not panic and continue trying to perform your best till the very end!

KEY CASE
INTERVIEW
FRAMEWORKS

common source of anxiety among consulting candidates is mastering the case interview. To add to this
anxiety, many consulting books and coaches teach
multiple different frameworks, each of which has a different
matrix or name to learn. However, it is incredibly hard to
master a handful of frameworks, much less twenty different
ones, in a short period of time. This chapter will help to consolidate the frameworks that you need to know into four key case
frameworks.

Before we dive into the four key case frameworks, you must
learn, and deeply understand, this one overarching principle:
**every single problem can be broken down into a simple cost-
benefit analysis.** The solution should always be the most net
positive or the least negative option. Using a simple mathematical illustration,

- Solution #1 to business problem = Pros
  - Cons = Highest positive score

- Solution #2 to business problem = Pros - Cons = High positive score

- Solution #3 to business problem = Pros - Cons = Negative score

When facing a business problem, every business owner or decision-maker is weighing the pros and cons of doing something. Should you do X or Y? What are the pros and cons? Which option gives me the best outcome? The five frameworks that we will go into are merely expansions of this concept. For example, take a new product launch case: what is the best way to launch a new product? To solve this, you are really weighing the pros and cons of each option. The quantitative sections are simply ways you can help to quantify the pros and cons of doing something - market sizing is a way to quantify what the potential volume, and therefore revenue and pro of entering that market.

The reason why you need to deeply understand and ingrain this simple cost-benefit analysis into all of your decision-making is because, while the five case frameworks are broadly applicable to the majority of case interviews, you will sometimes -- and this is becoming more and more commonplace today -- get a case interview where it does not fit into one of these case frameworks below. If that happens, you do not need to panic. Simply go back to the basic overarching principle: what are the pros and cons of doing an approach that could potentially solve this business problem?

Four Key Case Frameworks

The four key case frameworks are:

1. Profitability

2. New market or new product or growth

3. Pricing

4. Mergers and acquisitions

These are the four key case frameworks that apply to the majority of case interviews. You should memorize these frameworks, the bullet points under each driver, and know them like the back of your hand. The reason why you want to memorize these is because a case interview is stressful enough without you panicking about which framework to use and what could come under each bucket.

Profitability Framework

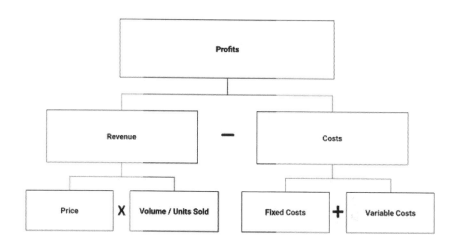

Profits = Revenue - Costs

- Revenue = Price x Volume / Units Sold

- Costs = Fixed Costs + Variable Costs
  (Variable Cost / Unit x Units Sold)

Declining profitability could be caused by changes to any driver within one of these buckets:

- Price: Lower prices

- Volume: Fewer units sold due to changes in the economy (recession ongoing), more competition, changes in consumer preferences, blockage in distribution channel, decline in consumer population over time,

- Fixed costs: Capital costs, rent, equipment costs, business insurance

- Variable costs: Labor costs (not contracted), supply and price of raw materials, distribution costs, sales commissions, advertising costs

New Market, New Product Or Growth Framework

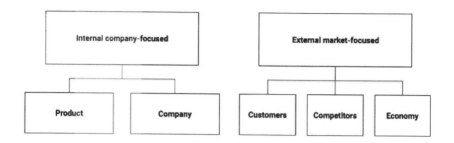

Product

- Product features: what are the benefits of this product, why would a consumer buy it

- Product differentiation: how is this product different from other products

- Product substitutes: what are the other options in the market

- Product price and packaging: how is this product priced and packaged, what is the price elasticity of this product, what is included in the product

- Product marketing: what are the channels to market this product, does the company already have a strong marketing presence in these channels or are these new channels that need to be set up

Company

- Leadership team: who is running this company, what are their strengths and weaknesses

- Financials: what is the financial situation of this company, are they able to fund entry into a new market or launch a new product

- Company goals: what are the revenue goals, what are the gross margin goals, how would this product or new market help the company achieve their goals

- Distribution channels: what are the ways this product is going to be launched into the market

Customers / market

- Target customer segments: who are the target customer segments, how quickly have these customer segments been growing year over year

- Customer trends: how are customer preferences trending, what are customers demanding

- Total Addressable Market (TAM): what is the TAM, is there applicability to launch this product outside of the US (or otherwise stated country) in the future, how does the global TAM look like, is the market continuing to grow (life cycle of market is emerging, mature or declining)

Competition

- Competitors: are there any competitors in the market, what does the competitor structure and market share look like (e.g., long tail of small competitors, monopoly, oligopoly)

- Barriers to entry: what are the barriers to entry posed by competitors, is there a high likelihood of a price war

- Competitor strategies: what are the

competitors doing, how are they targeting
customers and marketing their product

Economy

- State of economy: how is the economy performing,
  is there an ongoing recession or economic boom

After you have laid out this framework, if the decision is to go
ahead with launching a new product or entering a new market,
there are three fundamental approaches:

- Build: build from scratch

- Buy: acquire an existing product or company

- Partner: partner with a company

Pricing Framework

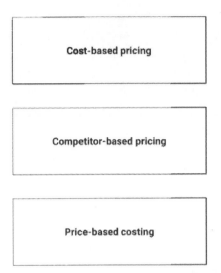

With any product, there are three ways to price it:

- Cost-based pricing: how much does it cost the company to produce this product, what is the breakeven point, what is the profit margin the company wants to earn on this product

- Competitor-based pricing: how are competitors' products priced, how does this product compare to competitors' products, how differentiated is the product, what will the competitive response be

- Price-based costing: what are consumers willing to pay for this product, at consumers' willingness to pay prices, will the company be able to make the profit margin that they want, what is this product worth to consumers, what are they currently paying for similar substitutes

Mergers And Acquisitions Framework

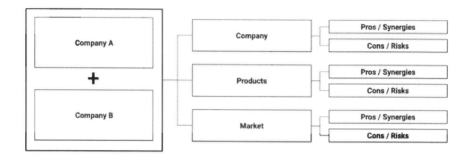

Decision to merge with or acquire a company = pros of M&A - cons of M&A = net positive

There are three main areas when considering an M&A:

- Company: are there efficiencies from combining operations (e.g., G&A, S&M), are there risks to cultural integration, are there efficiencies from combining distribution channels, are there tax advantages, how will shareholder value improve, are there synergies or risks from combining the management talent

- Products: will this diversify the product catalogue and/or cannibalize existing products, are the products from both companies compatible and synergistic (i.e., does one product fit a need that the other product requires), are there any R&D synergies or risks

- Market: will this M&A increase market share in a particular industry, how will competitors in the market respond, are there any legal or regulatory risks to the M&A

Using Case Frameworks Effectively

While it is recommended that you memorize these case frameworks, the most effective way to use case frameworks is to be flexible. You might have noticed that across these four key case frameworks, there are recurring categories:

- Product

  - Price

  - Volume

  - Costs

- Company

- Market / consumers

- Competitors

- Economy

These are the main categories that you should feel free to use and rearrange as needed to fit the case. Treat these categories and their associated sub-points as your key arsenal of business content. With these themes in mind, you will be able to tackle any business problem.

My goal with laying out a set of simple and effective case interview frameworks is to equip you with an all-around winning structure that is both easy to learn and easy to deploy. Many years ago, when I was studying case interview frameworks, I remember being extremely confused by the numerous case frameworks that each book would tell me I needed to learn: an Aristotelian framework, Porter's Five Forces, BCG matrix -- the list goes on and on. Later on, I realized that these ended up hurting my ability to answer case interviews effectively because there were so many competing case frameworks, and no clear instruction for when to use what.

By using the four key case interview frameworks that I have laid out in this chapter, and by understanding the one overarching principle that every single problem can be broken down into a simple cost-benefit analysis, I was able to grasp and respond to every single case interview that I came across.

PRACTICE

Armed with the knowledge from the previous chapters, the next step is to practice, and practice diligently and consistently. This is the most critical step in the interview preparation phase and truly cannot be emphasized enough. How much should you practice? How often should you practice?

This chapter will walk you through a few consulting interview preparation schedules that you can use to guide your own practice depending on how much time you have left and how much time you want to devote to this. A good rule of thumb for how much case practice you should do before your first consulting interview is completing and learning from at least 10 practice cases.

Calendar #1: 60-day Plan

Day	Time (hrs.)	Task(s)
1	1.0	• Read Chapter 1 (Introduction) and Chapter 2 (The Resume)
2	2.0	• Work on resume • Send resume to three friends or mentors for peer review

3	-	
4	-	
5	1.5	• Review comments from peer reviewers • Incorporate edits into resume • Send updated resume back to friends or mentors
6	-	
7	-	
8	1.0	• Review any additional comments from peer reviewers • Incorporate edits into resume • Review final resume and submit for application
9	-	
10	2.0	• Read Chapter 3 (The Interview Process) and Chapter 4 (The "Fit" or "Personal Experience Interview")
11	3.0	• Write out bullet point answers for the "fit" interview • Practice reading answers in front of a mirror or record oneself reading the answers
12	-	
13	3.0	• Grab a friend (ideally someone who has successfully been through the consulting process) to review your answers for the "fit" interview

		• Practice reading your refined answers in front of a mirror or record oneself reading the answers
14	-	
15	2.0	• Read Chapter 5 (The Case Interview) and Chapter 6 (The Key Case Interview Frameworks)
16	1.0	• Memorize the key case interview frameworks
17	-	
18	1.5	• Grab a friend or family member and do your first practice case • Jot down any learnings and areas to practice in your next case
19	-	
20	1.5	• Grab a friend or family member and do another practice case • Jot down any learnings and areas to practice in your next case
21	-	
22	1.5	• Grab a friend or family member and do another practice case • Jot down any learnings and areas to practice in your next case
23	-	
24	1.5	• Grab a friend or family member and do another practice case • Jot down any learnings and

		areas to practice in your next case
25	-	
26	1.5	• Grab a friend or family member and do another practice case • Jot down any learnings and areas to practice in your next case
27	-	
28	1.5	• Grab a friend or family member and do another practice case • Jot down any learnings and areas to practice in your next case
29	-	
30	-	
Every Other Day	1.5	• Grab a friend or family member and do another practice case • Jot down any learnings and areas to practice in your next case
58	1.5	• Grab a friend or family member and practice your "fit" stories and answers • Refine your "fit" stories and answers
59	1.5	• Grab a friend or family member and practice your "fit" stories and answers
60	-	

Calendar #2: 30-day Plan

Day	Time (hrs.)	Task(s)
1	1.0	• Read Chapter 1 (Introduction) and Chapter 2 (The Resume)
2	2.0	• Work on resume • Send resume to three friends or mentors for peer review
3	-	
4	-	
5	1.5	• Review comments from peer reviewers • Incorporate edits into resume • Send updated resume back to friends or mentors
6	-	
7	-	
8	1.0	• Review any additional comments from peer reviewers • Incorporate edits into resume • Review final resume and submit for application
9	-	
10	2.0	• Read Chapter 3 (The Interview Process) and Chapter 4 (The "Fit" or "Personal Experience Interview")
11	3.0	• Write out bullet point answers for the "fit" interview • Practice reading answers in front

		of a mirror or record oneself reading the answers
12	-	
13	-	
14	2.0	• Read Chapter 5 (The Case Interview) and Chapter 6 (The Key Case Interview Frameworks)
15	1.0	• Memorize the key case interview frameworks
16	-	
17	1.5	• Grab a friend or family member and do your first practice case • Jot down any learnings and areas to practice in your next case
18	-	
19	3.0	• Grab a friend or family member and do two practice cases spaced out (e.g., one in the morning, one in the afternoon) • Jot down any learnings and areas to practice in your next case
20	-	
21	3.0	• Grab a friend or family member and do two practice cases spaced out (e.g., one in the morning, one in the afternoon) • Jot down any learnings and areas to practice in your next case

22	-	
23	3.0	• Grab a friend or family member and do two practice cases spaced out (e.g., one in the morning, one in the afternoon) • Jot down any learnings and areas to practice in your next case
24	-	
25	3.0	• Grab a friend or family member and do two practice cases spaced out (e.g., one in the morning, one in the afternoon) • Jot down any learnings and areas to practice in your next case
26	-	
27	3.0	• Grab a friend or family member and do two practice cases spaced out (e.g., one in the morning, one in the afternoon) • Jot down any learnings and areas to practice in your next case
28	-	
29	1.5	• Grab a friend or family member and practice your "fit" stories and answers
30	-	

Calendar #3: Two-week Plan

Day	Time (hrs.)	Task(s)

1	3.0	• Read Chapter 1 (Introduction) and Chapter 2 (The Resume) • Work on resume • Send resume to three friends or mentors for peer review
2	3.0	• Review any additional comments from peer reviewers • Incorporate edits into resume • Review final resume and submit for application
3	2.0	• Read Chapter 3 (The Interview Process) and Chapter 4 (The "Fit" or "Personal Experience Interview")
4	3.0	• Write out bullet point answers for the "fit" interview • Practice reading answers in front of a mirror or record oneself reading the answers
5	2.0	• Read Chapter 5 (The Case Interview) and Chapter 6 (The Key Case Interview Frameworks)
6	1.5	• Grab a friend or family member and do one practice case • Jot down any learnings and areas to practice in your next case
7	3.0	• Grab a friend or family member and do two practice cases spaced out (e.g., one in the morning, one in the afternoon) • Jot down any learnings and areas to practice in your next case
8	1.5	• Grab a friend or family member

		and do one practice case ● Jot down any learnings and areas to practice in your next case
9	-	
10	3.0	● Grab a friend or family member and do two practice cases spaced out (e.g., one in the morning, one in the afternoon) ● Jot down any learnings and areas to practice in your next case
11	3.0	● Grab a friend or family member and do two practice cases spaced out (e.g., one in the morning, one in the afternoon) ● Jot down any learnings and areas to practice in your next case
12	1.5	● Grab a friend or family member and do one practice case ● Jot down any learnings and areas to practice in your next case
13	1.5	● Grab a friend or family member and do one practice case ● Jot down any learnings and areas to practice in your next case
14	-	

PRACTICE CASE INTERVIEWS

T his chapter is broken down into five sections along the key case interview frameworks covered earlier:

- Profitability

- New market, new product or growth

- Pricing

- Merger and acquisition

- Other cases

Before you dive into the practice cases, let us revisit the case interview format. As mentioned earlier, the case interview format requires practice. The practice cases in this chapter are structured in a question and answer manner for clarity. However, when working on the practice cases in this chapter, you should always be cognizant of and practicing this format. Let us try it out with the first practice case.

Profitability

Trader Goods Grocery Store (case interview format)

- Interviewer: Imagine that our client is a national grocery store chain called Trader Goods that has been seeing declining profits over the past two years. In the past year, their "ready-to-go" department, which sells fresh, ready-to-eat meals has been reporting severe losses. This department sells fresh, already cooked soups, sandwiches, mix-and-match dishes, and sushi. Prior to that, low-price competitors such as Walmart, Safeway, and the like have been eroding margins in the traditional grocery business.

- Candidate: [furiously jots down notes on the case study problem]

- Interviewer: [provides rest of the case study problem and stops] Our client has asked us to figure out why profits have been declining and what they should do to turn things around.

- Candidate: Great, can I ask you a couple of clarifying questions?

- Interviewer: Yes, go ahead

- Candidate: [asks a clarifying question] You mentioned that the client has been experiencing declining profits, is that correct?

- Interviewer: Yes

- Candidate: [asks a probing question] Is there any additional information about whether other departments, aside from the "ready-to-go" department, are experiencing declining profitability or losses as well?

- Interviewer: No

- Candidate: Okay great, thank you

- Interviewer: [asks the first case question]
  What do you think are potential main drivers
  for Trader Goods' declining profits?

- Candidate: [asks for some time, usually 30 to 120 seconds]
  Can I take a few moments to lay out my thoughts?

- Interviewer: Yes, go ahead

- [90 seconds later...]

- Candidate: [provides structure to answer the first
  question] First, I would identify which department
  is experiencing declining profits. Profits can be
  understood as taking Revenue minus Costs. Breaking
  that down even further, Revenue equals to Price
  multiplied by Volume or Units Sold. Costs, on the
  other hand, is the summation of Fixed Costs and
  Variable Costs, which can be further broken down into
  Variable Cost per Unit multiplied by Units Sold.

- Let me share the main drivers under each of these buckets,

  - For Price, Trader Foods might have had to lower
    prices to compete with low-price competitors
    like Walmart, which squeezed their profits.

  - Under Volume, there could be a couple of drivers.
    First, there could be fewer units sold due to increasing
    competition from low-price competitors who
    entered the grocery store space. Second, there could
    have been potential environmental reasons which

has led to fewer units sold such as a pandemic, which would impact the "ready-to-eat" department due to fears about contamination and the situation where more people are at home and have more time to eat. Third, there could have been a change in consumer tastes away from sandwiches, etc., and towards more healthy options such as salads, smoothies, and juices. Lastly, the market could be a declining market potentially from the rise of online grocery shopping.

o   In terms of Fixed costs, the client could have seen higher rent costs in recent years and/or higher equipment costs, potentially from having to replace old or malfunctioning equipment.

o   In terms of Variable costs, the client could have experienced higher labor costs in recent years, potentially from stronger union power, and/or higher price of raw materials and/or goods sold in the grocery store, which would drive up the cost of goods sold, and lower gross profits. There could also have been higher advertising costs from having to differentiate itself against competitors more.

•   Interviewer: [moves on to second question] Great, after reviewing the profits for the "ready-to-go" department, the team believes that a key cause of profitability is the declining volume of units sold. What are the most likely reasons for this? The client has also provided this table of food sold.

Volume of units sold

Food item	2017	2018	2019	2020
Fried chicken	550,000	75,000	43,000	20,000

Sushi	20,000	20,000	21,000	22,000
Soups	10,000	10,000	12,000	20,000
Salads	20,000	50,000	130,000	200,000
Sandwiches	70,000	45,000	33,000	27,000
Pizza	300,000	110,000	80,000	50,000

- Candidate: [asks for some time again] Let me take some time to look through the data

- [60 seconds later...]

- Candidate: [provides structured answer to second question] Looking at this table, the food items that have declining volume of units sold are: fried chicken, sandwiches, and pizza. The food items that have increasing volume of units sold are: sushi, soups, and salads.

- There could be a few potential reasons for these trends. First, there could have been a change in consumer preferences towards healthier options. The marked decrease in traditionally perceived "less healthy" options such as fried chicken and pizza, and the significant increase in salads, soups, and sushi suggests that there could be a change in consumer tastes. Second, there could have been potential health concerns around chicken. The significant and sharp drop in fried chicken purchases suggest that there could have been a related health concern around chicken, such as chicken viruses or major contamination issues with chicken, etc.

- Interviewer: [moves on to third question] Got it. After reviewing the data, the team finds that the gross profit of each unit sold of these products has not changed for the past three years. The client has provided this table of gross profit per unit sold. Which food item(s) have driven the greatest decline in total gross profit?

Food item	Gross profit per unit sold
Fried chicken	$4
Sushi	$7
Soups	$8
Salads	$15
Sandwiches	$15
Pizza	$10

- Candidate: [asks for some time again] Let me take a few seconds to organize my thoughts

- [60 seconds later...]

- Candidate: [provides structured answer to third question] We can calculate the loss in gross profit from this data and the data provided earlier. For fried chicken, we can take the previous volume sold, 550,000 units, minus the current volume sold, 20,000 units, and then multiply that by the gross profit per unit of fried chicken, which is $4. This gets us to a loss of approximately $2,100,000. For sandwiches, the loss in gross profit is (70,000 - 27,000)*15 which gives us approximately $600,000. For pizza, the loss in gross profit is (300,000 - 50,000)*10 which gives us $2,500,000. As such, the biggest loss in gross profit comes from pizza, followed by fried chicken, and then sandwiches.

- Interviewer: [moves on to fourth question] I see. Now, after you have done all this analysis, what are some recommendations for turning around the business?

- Candidate: [asks for some time again] Let me take some time to write down some thoughts

- [60 seconds later...]

- Candidate: [provides structured answer to fourth question] I can think of a couple of potential recommendations for Trader Goods. First, they could boost demand and sales in high gross profit food items that are growing (e.g., salad) through more advertising and promotion. Next, they could investigate innovating and reinventing "healthier" food items such as selling gluten-free sandwiches or cauliflower crust pizza, etc. Thirdly, they could create a custom made-to-order section for "ready-to-go" food so that consumers can pick and choose what ingredients they want in their sushi, sandwiches, pizzas, etc. Fourth, they could move towards offering more "healthier" food options such as a smoothie and juice bar, fresh cut fruits selection, etc. Lastly, they could raise prices on food items that have been declining (e.g., fried chicken, sandwiches, pizza) assuming that the current base of consumers who have not switched away from these food items find them relatively price inelastic.

- Interviewer: [moves on to fifth question] Got it. Now imagine that you have a meeting with the CEO of Trader Goods, and you are asked to share a summary of your findings to date. What would you say?

- Candidate: [asks for some time again] Let me take some time to gather my thoughts

- [60 seconds later...]

- Candidate: [provides structured answer to last question] Trader Goods has been experiencing declining profits over the last few years, mainly driven by significant drops in volume of units sold in the "ready-to-go" section of certain food items, such as pizza, fried chicken, and sandwiches. Conversely, some other food items, such as sushi, salads, and soups have been seeing an increase in volume of units sold.

- These trends were determined to be mainly driven by a significant change in consumer tastes towards healthier food options. As consumers have become more health-conscious and educated about food and nutrition, they have begun to look for healthier options.

- As such, we would recommend that Trader Goods improve profitability in the "ready-to-go" department by implementing five strategies. First, they could boost demand and sales in high gross profit food items that are growing (e.g., salad) through more advertising and promotion. Next, they could investigate innovating and reinventing "healthier" food items such as selling gluten-free sandwiches or cauliflower crust pizza, etc. Thirdly, they could create a custom made-to-order section for "ready-to-go" food so that consumers can pick and choose what ingredients they want in their sushi, sandwiches, pizzas, etc. Fourth, they could move towards offering more "healthier" food options such as a smoothie and juice bar, fresh cut fruits selection, etc. Lastly, they could raise prices on food items that have been declining (e.g., fried chicken, sandwiches, pizza) assuming that the current base of consumers who have not switched away from these food items find them relatively price inelastic.

- We would need to further investigate the ROI of each of these initiatives to prioritize resourcing and implementation.

- [Case ends when all questions are asked and answered]

Trader Goods Grocery Store (question and answer structure)

Problem statement

Our client is a national grocery store chain called Trader Goods that has been seeing declining profits over the past two years. In the past year, their "ready-to-go" department, which sells fresh, ready-to-eat meals has been reporting severe losses. This department sells fresh, already cooked soups, sandwiches, mix-and-match dishes, and sushi. Prior to that, low-price competitors such as Walmart, Safeway, and the like have been eroding margins in the traditional grocery business.

Our client has asked us to figure out why profits have been declining and what they should do to turn things around.

Question 1: What do you think are potential main drivers for Trader Goods' declining profits?

Firstly, identify which department is experiencing declining profits.

Profits = Revenue - Costs

- Revenue = Price x Volume / Units Sold

- Costs = Fixed Costs + Variable Costs (Variable Cost / Unit x Units Sold)

Under each of these buckets,

- Price:

  o Trader Foods might have had to lower prices to compete with low-price competitors like Walmart, which squeezed their profits

- Volume:

  - Fewer units sold due to increasing competition from low-price competitors who entered the grocery store space

  - Potential environmental reasons which has led to fewer units sold such as a pandemic, which would impact the "ready-to-eat" department due to fears about contamination and the situation where more people are at home and have more time to eat

  - Change in consumer tastes away from sandwiches, etc., and towards more healthy options such as salads, smoothies, and juices

  - Declining market or category potentially from the rise of online grocery shopping

- Fixed costs:

  - Higher rent costs in recent years

  - Higher equipment costs, potentially from having to replace old or malfunctioning equipment

- Variable costs:

  - Higher labor costs in recent years, potentially from stronger union power

  - Higher price of raw materials and/or goods sold in the grocery store, which would drive up the cost of goods sold, and lower gross profits

  - Higher advertising costs from having to differentiate itself against competitors more

Question 2: After reviewing the profits for the "ready-to-go" department, the team believes that a key cause of profitability is the declining volume of units sold. What are the most likely reasons for this?

Food item	Volume of units sold			
	2017	2018	2019	2020
Fried chicken	550,000	75,000	43,000	20,000
Sushi	20,000	20,000	21,000	22,000
Soups	10,000	10,000	12,000	20,000
Salads	20,000	50,000	130,000	200,000
Sandwiches	70,000	45,000	33,000	27,000
Pizza	300,000	110,000	80,000	50,000

Looking at this table,

- Food items that have declining volume of units sold are:

  o Fried chicken

  o Sandwiches

  o Pizza

- Food items that have increasing volume of units sold are:

  o Sushi

    o   Soups

    o   Salads

- Potential reasons for these trends are:

- Change in consumer preferences towards healthier options. The marked decrease in traditionally perceived "less healthy" options such as fried chicken and pizza, and the significant increase in salads, soups, and sushi suggests that there could be a change in consumer tastes

- Potential health concerns around chicken. The significant and sharp drop in fried chicken purchases suggest that there could have been a related health concern around chicken, such as chicken viruses or major contamination issues with chicken, etc.

Question 3: After reviewing the data, the team finds that the gross profit of each unit sold of these products has not changed for the past three years. Which food item(s) have driven the greatest decline in total gross profit?

Food item	Gross profit per unit sold
Fried chicken	$4
Sushi	$7
Soups	$8
Salads	$15
Sandwiches	$15
Pizza	$10

Loss in gross profit:

- Fried chicken: (550,000 - 20,000)*4
  = 530,000 * 4 = ~$2,100,000

- Sandwiches: (70,000 - 27,000)*15
  = 43,000 * 15 = ~$600,000

- Pizza: (300,000 - 50,000)*10 =
  250,000 * 10 = $2,500,000

The biggest loss in gross profit comes from pizza, followed by fried chicken, and then sandwiches.

Question 4: What are some recommendations for turning around the business?

- Boost demand and sales in high gross profit food items that are growing (e.g., salad) through more advertising and promotion

- Innovating and reinventing "healthier" food items such as selling gluten-free sandwiches or cauliflower crust pizza, etc.

- Creating a custom made-to-order section for "ready-to-go" food so that consumers can pick and choose what ingredients they want in their sushi, sandwiches, pizzas, etc.

- Move towards offering more "healthier" food options such as a smoothie and juice bar, fresh cut fruits selection, etc.

- Raising prices on food items that have been declining (e.g., fried chicken, sandwiches, pizza) if the current base of consumers who have not switched away from these food items find them relatively price inelastic

Question 5: You have a meeting with the CEO of Trader Goods, and you are asked to share a summary of your findings to date. What would you say?

Trader Goods has been experiencing declining profits over the last few years, mainly driven by significant drops in volume of units sold in the "ready-to-go" section of certain food items, such as pizza, fried chicken, and sandwiches. Conversely, some other food items, such as sushi, salads, and soups have been seeing an increase in volume of units sold.

These trends were determined to be mainly driven by a significant change in consumer tastes towards healthier food options. As consumers have become more health-conscious and educated about food and nutrition, they have begun to look for healthier options.

As such, we would recommend that Trader Goods improve profitability in the "ready-to-go" department by implementing five strategies:

- Boost demand and sales in high gross profit food items that are growing (e.g., salad) through more advertising and promotion

- Innovating and reinventing "healthier" food items such as selling gluten-free sandwiches or cauliflower crust pizza, etc.

- Creating a custom made-to-order section for "ready-to-go" food so that consumers can pick and choose what ingredients they want in their sushi, sandwiches, pizzas, etc.

- Move towards offering more "healthier" food options such

as a smoothie and juice bar, fresh cut fruits selection, etc.

- Raising prices on food items that have been declining (e.g., fried chicken, sandwiches, pizza) if the current base of consumers who have not switched away from these food items find them relatively price inelastic

We would need to further investigate the ROI of each of these initiatives to prioritize resourcing and implementation.

Tasty Meats

Problem statement

Our client is Tasty Meats, who is one of the largest meat producers in the U.S. They buy livestock from farmers, process the meat, and pack the meat for delivery to customers, who are major supermarket chains and grocery stores in the U.S.

The beef industry used to have many small meat producers. However, in the past ten years, the beef industry went through a rapid consolidation phase. Tasty Meats grew very rapidly through the successful acquisition and turnaround of smaller, failing beef producers. However, over the last three years, profitability for Tasty Meats has declined significantly. The CEO has brought our team in to determine the reason behind declining profits and how they can best fix it.

Question 1: What key areas would you want to investigate to determine the reasons for Tasty Meats' declining profits?

Firstly, identify which department is experiencing declining profits.

Profits = Revenue - Costs

- Revenue = Price x Volume / Units Sold

- Costs = Fixed Costs + Variable Costs
  (Variable Cost / Unit x Units Sold)

Under each of these buckets,

- Volume:
    - Volumes may fall due to a shift in consumer food

preferences (e.g., more vegetarianism, veganism)

- o Volumes may have also fallen due to food scares (e.g., mad cow disease) or health concerns around consuming too much beef (e.g., high cholesterol)

- Price:

  - o Prices may be under ongoing consumer and supermarket pressure

  - o Product mix may be shifting to lower priced meat cuts (e.g., chicken)

- Variable costs:

  - o Raw materials cost, mainly due to livestock

  - o Labor costs of operating the factories and machinery

  - o Distribution costs of delivering the meats to various supermarkets and grocery stores

- Fixed costs:

  - o Capital costs include factories which process the meats

  - o Equipment costs from purchase to maintenance and renewal. If equipment assets are aging, maintenance and renewal costs would go up

Question 2: From the data that the client has provided, one of the potential causes for their declining profits is their high meat processing cost. What are the most likely reasons for the higher processing cost per cow for Tasty Meats?

	Meat processing data	
Site	Average number of cows processed per month per site	Average processing cost per cow
Tasty Meats	300,000	$0.60
Possible Beef	600,000	$0.20

- Different operational processes: Tasty Meats might be using old and slower equipment or manual processes (e.g., hand processing and packing)

- Higher labor costs: Tasty Meats might have more contracted employees (potentially due to more manual operational processes) and/or have to pay higher wages due to stronger union power or more expensive geographical locations

- Type of beef: Tasty Meats might be processing different types of cows (e.g., larger) or different parts of the cow (e.g., tongue) which makes it harder to process efficiently

- Factory size: Possible Beef might have larger factories and therefore higher economies of scale compared to Tasty Meats. If Tasty Meats acquired a lot of smaller players, they might be operating in many smaller factories versus a few larger factories

- Higher fixed costs: Tasty Meats might have older factories and older machinery, which could have more expensive maintenance and renewal costs

- Type of packaging: Tasty Meats might be packaging their beef for more premium, high-end sales and be using more expensive raw materials (e.g., waxed paper)

Question 3: How would you determine which of these potential reasons is the main driver(s)?

- Conduct primary and secondary research through:

  - Interviews with Tasty Meats employees

  - Industry experts

  - Public industry reports and company annual reports, if available

  - Newspaper articles

- Gather information on:

  - Age of factories and equipment

  - Operational processes

  - Number of employees

  - Salaries of employees

  - Location of factories

Question 4: The team has determined that the average price per pound for Tasty Meats meat has also fallen significantly in the last few years. What are potential reasons for the falling prices?

- Customer

  - Demand for beef may have fallen leading to high supply and low demand (e.g., more vegetarianism, veganism, health scares around beef)

- ○ Shift in product mix to cheaper cuts of beef

- Economy

  - ○ Ongoing recession leading to lower consumers' willingness to pay and more aggressive bargaining

- Competitors

  - ○ More U.S. competitors entering the U.S. beef industry leading to lower prices

  - ○ Introduction of a price war by either Tasty Meats or one of the competitors

  - ○ Reduction in barriers to entry in the beef industry by international beef companies (e.g., easier for U.K. beef producers to export beef to U.S.)

- Company

  - ○ Poor negotiation with Tasty Meats' customers, which are supermarkets and grocery stores

  - ○ Change in pricing strategy in a bid to boost revenue

Question 5: The team discovers that demand has grown for specialty cuts (e.g., beef tongue) but fallen for conventional cuts (e.g., minced beef). Since a year ago, retailers' monthly order volume for specialty cuts have increased by 30% while orders for conventional cuts have decreased by 20%. In addition, prices per pound to retailers for specialty cuts have increased by 50% but decreased by 20% for conventional cuts. What is the change in monthly revenue from a year ago?

	One year ago	
	Specialty cuts	**Conventional cuts**
Monthly volume	5,000,000 pounds	10,000,000 pounds
Price per pound to retailers	$1.00	$0.50

- A year ago:

  - Revenue = 5m x $1.00 + 10m x $0.50 = $10m

- Today:

  - Revenue = (5m x 130%) x ($1.00 x 150%) + (10m x 80%) x ($0.50 x 80%) = 6.5m x $1.50 + 8m x $0.40 = ~$10m + $3.2m = ~$13.2m

Question 6: The CEO of Tasty Meats convenes a meeting to discuss the team's findings so far and what they should do to turn things around. What would you tell the CEO?

Tasty Meats has experienced declining profits from two main drivers: (1) higher meat processing costs, and (2) lower average prices per pound of meat.

We would recommend doing the following:

- Consolidate the production of smaller factories to achieve economies of scale and maximize production capacity

- Potentially move production to lower cost geographic areas and hire workers at lower cost (without strong union influence, etc.)

- Increase production of specialty cuts that has been experiencing strong demand recently

- Hire business talent to lead negotiations with retailers to improve average sale price per pound

- Explore exporting beef to other countries if the ROI looks positive

We would need to further investigate the ROI of each of these initiatives to prioritize resourcing and implementation.

Haven Healthcare

Problem statement

Our client is Haven Healthcare, a healthcare company in the Pacific Northwest. It is both a provider and payor, meaning that it provides both healthcare services and health insurance services. Employers pay Haven Healthcare an insurance premium to cover its employees, and, in return, employees can go to Haven Healthcare when necessary to receive healthcare services, such as surgeries, hospitalization, routine check-ups, etc.

Haven Healthcare currently has a million employees enrolled in its healthcare insurance plan. It has 500 salaried physicians who provide both primary and specialty care in its 10 hospitals in the Pacific Northwest. When a patient chooses to seek healthcare outside of Haven Healthcare's network of hospitals and physicians, Haven Healthcare pays the respective out-of-network physician on a fee-for-service rate that has been negotiated and agreed upon.

Over the past year, Haven Healthcare has been experiencing declining profits. Haven's CEO has hired our team to help determine what is causing the declining profits and how to turn things around.

Question 1: What key areas do you think might be driving Haven Healthcare's decline in profitability?

Firstly, identify which department is experiencing declining profits.

Profits = Revenue - Costs

- Revenue = Price x Volume / Units Sold

- Costs = Fixed Costs + Variable Costs
  (Variable Cost / Unit x Units Sold)

Under each of these buckets,

- Price: Lower insurance premiums

- Volume: Fewer patients visiting the hospital
  or lower efficiency in serving patients so fewer
  patients are treated in the same amount of time

- Fixed costs: Hospital costs, equipment costs

- Variable costs: Drugs, outpatient care, external network
  fee-for-service costs, internal physician salaries,
  hospital administrative staff costs, higher medical
  costs for treating higher risk patient demographics

Question 2: After reviewing some client data, the team believes that one of the drivers is the high external network referral costs. What are the most likely reasons why the average cost for out-of-network referrals are higher than St. Luke's Healthcare?

	Number of patients	Average cost of out-of-network referral (per member per month)
Haven Healthcare	1,000,000	$300
St. Luke's Health-care	5,000,000	$200

- Poor negotiation with out-of-network physicians:
  St. Luke's might have negotiated better rates
  through more effective negotiations

- Lower number of referrals: Haven has a smaller number of patients and, as a result, might have weaker negotiating power and less leverage than St. Luke's Healthcare

- High risk mix of patients: Haven might have a significantly higher number of patients who are high risk patients (e.g., older patients, chronically ill patients, etc.)

- Mix of referral specialties needed: Haven might need a mix of specialties, which are generally more expensive (e.g., orthopedics, neurosurgery, cardiology), while St. Luke's might need a mix of specialties which are generally less expensive (e.g., family medicine, pediatrics)

Question 3: The team finds that Haven is paying a significantly high referral cost for its orthopedic patients. They have gathered the following data on Haven's orthopedic patient population:

- **Haven has 1,000,000 patients**

- **30% of its patients are 60 years or older**

Additional data only provided when asked:

- **The prevalence of orthopedic problems in the 60+ years old population is 40%**

- **The prevalence of orthopedic problems in the <60 years old population is 10%**

- **Haven Healthcare currently has orthopedic doctors who can provide services for about 50% of orthopedic cases (mainly the less serious ones)**

How many orthopedic patient referrals does Haven Healthcare

provide each year?

- 60+ years old population: 1,000,000
  x 30% x 40% = 120,000

- <60 years old population: 1,000,000
  x 70% x 10% = 70,000

- Orthopedic referrals = (120,000 + 70,000)
  x 50% = 95,000 referrals per year

Question 4: The team digs deeper and finds that Haven had estimated only 20,000 orthopedic referrals per year and had negotiated referral rates using that estimate. Why might Haven's orthopedic referrals be significantly higher than it had previously estimated?

- Increased prevalence of orthopedic problems in Haven's patient population due to increasingly large aging population

- Patients are demanding referrals to more specialized orthopedic physicians

- Haven's physicians are referring too many patients to specialists, even if the patients do not have serious orthopedic illnesses

- There are no clear guidelines for when physicians should be referring orthopedic patients to other specialists versus try to treat them in Haven's systems

- There are no incentives or penalties to guide physician behavior in terms of referrals

Question 5: Haven's CEO thinks that one potential idea

for reducing the number of orthopedic referrals to out-of-network physicians is to introduce an incentive plan for Haven's physicians. His plan is to provide:

- A $4 million incentive that is spread out among Haven's physicians if the target reduction of referrals is hit

- A $200,000 bonus to the top 10 physicians with the lowest orthopedic referral rates

What is the breakeven point in terms of referral reductions for Haven to recoup the cost of the incentive plan?

- Cost of referral (from question 2) = $300

- Cost of incentive plan = $4m + $2m = $6m

- Number of referrals to breakeven = $6m / $300 = 20,000 referrals

Haven will need to reduce the number of orthopedic referrals by 20,000 to recoup the cost of the incentive plan. This is an approximate 20% reduction off the base of 95,000 annual referrals currently.

Question 6: Your team has a meeting with Haven's CEO and CFO about the turnaround plan. Haven's CFO looks at the calculations and says that the healthcare system does not have the budget to implement this incentive plan at the moment and asks for other recommendations that do not straight their budget. What would you say?

We would look at ways to change the behavior of Haven's patients and physicians.

- Change patient behavior:

  - Put up posters in the hospital about the qualifications and experience of Haven's orthopedic doctors

  - Provide health and wellness education to Haven's patients on how to keep their bones and joints healthy

- Change physician behavior:

  - Create clear guidelines for when physicians should be referring orthopedic patients to other specialists

  - Institute penalties for physicians who are found to be wrongly referring patients

  - Institute a peer review committee charged with approving all orthopedic referrals

New Market, New Product Or Growth

Posters Printing Co.

Problem statement

Your client is Posters Printing Co., a leading manufacturer of specialty poster material that is sold to commercial printers to the production of campaign posters, banners, shop signs, and the like. Posters Printing Co. produces commercial posters and signs that can be used in a variety of applications and are very durable. Posters Printing Co. has been profitable over the past decade, but the business has stopped growing over the past 2 years. The CEO of Posters Printing Co. has asked our team to identify opportunities for growth.

Question 1: What do you think are potential reasons for why Posters Printing Co. has stopped growing over the past 2 years?

- Product

  - Increasing proliferation of product substitutes in the market in the last 2 years which have substantially decreased the number of products sold

- Company

  - Potential change in leadership team, which has led to lower efficiency in sales and/or operations, etc. (e.g., selling less to retailers or producing less)

  - Change in company goals to focus more on gross margin goals over revenue goals

- Customers / market

  - Change in consumer needs and preferences as consumers might have moved away from using posters for marketing or display, and moved toward digital options

  - Poster market is a mature market and TAM limits have been reached

  - Customer segment has been shrinking year over year

- Competition

  - Increasing number of competitors in the market who have been taking market share away from Posters Printing Co.

  - Competitors have been aggressively targeting customers and marketing new poster types (e.g., high resolution images, more diversity of colors, self-adhesive posters, etc.), successfully attracting them away from our client

- Economy

  - Ongoing recession and businesses have not been marketing and purchasing posters as frequently as previously

Question 2: The team finds that the change in customer preferences and increasingly inefficient company operations have caused growth to stall. While the company is still operating profitably, they have not added new sales and profits. What would you recommend that the client do?

Assuming the client is not capacity constrained or financially constrained, they could look into the following recommendations:

- Re-evaluate the way operations are configured to serve existing and potential customers to decrease the time lag for delivering services to new customers

- Understand what exactly what customer preferences are shifting towards; for example, if vinyl posters are desired, offer them, to address that growing customer segment

- Adjust incentives for operational staff to encourage higher efficiency

- Examine if existing machinery or equipment is a driver for lower efficiency and either repair or replace the equipment

- Create clear guidelines and checklists for company operations to improve throughput

Question 3: The client believes that the vinyl poster market is the new area of growth in this industry. They have asked you to estimate what the opportunity for vinyl posters is. This is the data that the team has:

- There are approximately 30,000 commercial printers in the U.S.

- The client has been the monopoly producer for paper posters and serves approximately 50% of small businesses, and 10% of medium and large businesses

- The average price for a paper poster is $500. The average price for a vinyl poster is estimated to be

40% of the price of producing a paper poster

How would you go about calculating this opportunity?

Market opportunity for vinyl posters:

- = number of businesses who will purchase vinyl posters

- = number of small, medium, and large businesses who will purchase vinyl posters

- = ~number of small, medium, and large businesses who are likely to purchase vinyl posters

To get to this number, you need to make certain assumptions about the number of small, medium, and large businesses in the U.S.:

- Assume there are about 3 million small and medium businesses, and 20,000 large businesses in the U.S.

Then, you need to figure out how many of these small, medium, and large businesses are likely to purchase vinyl posters:

- Assume that 50% of businesses who have purchased paper posters are likely to move to vinyl posters

- Assume that 20% of businesses who have not purchased paper posters before are likely to try vinyl posters

- Assume 50% of small & medium businesses have tried paper posters before = 50% x 3 million = 1.5 million

- Assume 80% of large businesses have tried paper posters before = 80% x 20,000 = 16,000

- Number of businesses who have not tried paper posters before:

- o Small & medium businesses = 3 million
  - 1.5 million = 1.5 million

- o Large businesses = 20,000 - 16,000 = 4,000

- Calculations for assuming that 50% of businesses who have purchased paper posters are likely to move to vinyl posters

  - o Small & medium businesses = 50% x 3 million = 1.5 million

  - o Large businesses = 16,000 x 50% = 8,000

- Calculations for assuming that 20% of businesses who have not purchased paper posters before are likely to try vinyl posters

  - o Small & medium businesses =1.5 million x 20% = 0.3 million

  - o Large businesses = 4,000 x 20% = 800

- Total no. of new businesses using vinyl posters

  - o Small & medium businesses =1.5 million + 0.3 million = 1.8 million

  - o Large businesses = 8,000 + 800 = 8,800

- Assume average spend differs by business size:

  - o Small & medium businesses avg. poster spend is $10,000

  - o Large businesses avg. poster spend is $5 million

- Total opportunity size = 1.8 million x $1,000 +

8,800 x $5 million= $1.8B + $4.4B = $6.2B

Note: Many of these numbers are assumptions. Any reasonable number assumption will be accepted.

Question 4: The CEO of Posters Printing Co. drops by the team room and asks for a quick update on what the team has found. What would you say?

Posters Printing Co. has seen stagnant growth because of two main reasons: (1) a change in customer preferences towards vinyl posters, and (2) increasingly inefficient company operations that have caused delayed delivery times and slower production of goods.

We would recommend prioritizing investing in entering the vinyl poster market, which is sized at approximately $6B. Posters Printing Co. has already built a solid reputation in the posters industry and currently maintains a monopoly lead. To continue growing and capturing customer demand, we must move quickly and gain a first-movers advantage in the vinyl poster market.

In parallel, we would also recommend increasing operational efficiency by:

- Re-evaluating the way operations are configured to serve existing and potential customers to decrease the time lag for delivering services to new customers

- Adjust incentives for operational staff to encourage higher efficiency

- Examine if existing machinery or equipment is a driver for lower efficiency and either repair or replace the equipment

- Create clear guidelines and checklists for
  company operations to improve throughput

We believe that we can improve growth significantly through these two approaches. We will need to further investigate the root causes of operational efficiency to identify which solution will directly address the slowdown as well.

Retin Aid Pharmaceuticals Company

Problem statement

Our client is a large pharmaceutical company that is preparing to launch a new product called Retin Aid. Retin Aid is a skin-care product derived from Vitamin A, also known as retinoid, to improve collagen production in the skin. The company plans to market Retin Aid to women as well as mature men who are interested in reducing wrinkles and improving the elasticity of their skin.

The current substitute product in the market is Botox injections, which have to be approved and administered by a doctor in the clinic. The skin effects are the same. However, these two products work in different ways. Retin Aid is a facial oil that can be applied at home and it encourages skin cells to ramp up their production of collagen and has no long-term negative effects. Botox freezes the facial muscles to eliminate the appearance of wrinkles, and Botox is derived from a toxin, which some dermatologists have purported to be dangerous for consumers.

Our client has asked us to assess the potential size of the market for this new product and to determine what are the best ways to launch this product into the market.

Question 1: How would you size the market for Retin Aid?

First, define the size of the market over a specific amount of time:

- Size of market over one year = number of customers x number of purchases per customer per year x price of each purchase

Let us tackle each component one by one. What is the price of Retin Aid? (Interviewer provides data point of $200)

To determine the number of customers:

- Assume that the product will only be launched in the U.S. given that all the clinical trials were held in the U.S. and it has been certified thus far by the FDA only

- The U.S. population is 320 million. The client believes that this product will target both women and mature men.

- Women population:

  o Assume women population is half of the U.S. population = 320 million x 50% = 160 million

  o Assume only women who are starting to experience the effects of aging would be interested in this product, which is the similar target group for Botox, and assume that women who are 40+ years old start using Botox, which is about half of the women population (assuming 80 years lifespan) = 160 million x 50% = 80 million

  o Assume that 80% of women in their forties and fifties are going to be interested in improving their appearance = (80 million / 2) x 80% = 32 million

  o Assume that only half of women in their sixties and seventies are going to be interested in improving their appearance = (80 million / 2) x 50% = 20 million

  o Assume that half of women in their thirties are going to be interested in preventing wrinkles and starting anti-aging skincare early = (160 million / 8) x 50% = 10 million

- o   Total number of women who would potentially use this product to improve their appearance = 32 million + 20 million + 10 million = 62 million

- o   Another factor to consider is ability to purchase. Of the 62 million women who might be interested in this product to improve their appearance, at the current price point of $200 per purchase, assume only 20% of this subset of women would be able to purchase this product = 62 million x 20% = 12.4 million

- o   A container of Retin Aid is expected to last an individual 3 months. Assuming that half of the women end up repurchasing while the other half do not = ~6 million x (12 months / 3 months) + ~6 million = ~24 million + ~6 million = ~30 million Retin Aid products sold a year

- Mature men population:

  - o   Assume men population is half of the U.S. population = 320 million x 50% = 160 million

  - o   Assume mature men means men who are in their fifties and sixties = (160 million / 8) x 2 = 40 million

  - o   Assume that only a quarter of men in their fifties and sixties are going to be interested in improving their appearance = 40 million / 4 = 10 million

  - o   Another factor to consider is ability to purchase. Of the 10 million men who might be interested in this product to improve their appearance, at the current price point of $200 per purchase, assume only 20% of this subset of men would be able to purchase this product = 10 million x 20% = 2 million

- A container of Retin Aid is expected to last an individual 3 months. Assuming that half of the men end up repurchasing while the other half do not = 1 million x (12 months / 3 months) + 1 million = 4 million + 1 million = 5 million Retin Aid products sold a year

- Total Addressable Market Opportunity:

  - Total estimated number of Retin Aid products sold a year = 30 million + 5 million = 35 million

  - Total estimated revenue from Retin Aid sales = 35 million x $200 = $7B

Question 2: What are the best ways to launch Retin Aid into the market?

Since Retin Aid has already been developed by the client, the next step is to figure out how to market and sell this product:

- Understand consumer needs and design marketing campaign language to directly target those needs

- Identify most effective marketing channels for similar skincare products (e.g., word-of-mouth / referral, paid ads, billboards, events, etc.)

- If the client does not have their own marketing team or relevant marketing expertise, partner with marketing agencies to help support these efforts

- Partner with key stakeholders, such as dermatologists, primary care doctors, etc. who are decision makers in prescribing this product

Question 3: The CEO calls for a meeting and asks what the team has discovered so far. What would you tell the CEO?

We believe that there is a huge market opportunity of $7B for Retin Aid through sizing consumer demand and willingness to purchase among women and mature men. The best ways to launch Retin Aid into the market are to:

- Design a marketing campaign that directly addresses consumer needs and uses the highest ROI marketing channels for skincare products

- Form strategic partnerships with key stakeholders, such as dermatologists, primary care doctors, etc., who are decision makers in prescribing this product

Additional research is needed to more effectively determine which marketing channels to go into based on their historical ROI and payback periods (i.e., how much time it takes for a marketing investment to pay off), as well as figure out which stakeholders are most influential in making the decision to promote and use this product.

Ortho-K Contact Lens

Problem statement

Our client is a large glasses company that has been producing glasses and sunglasses for the past decade. Their customers today are both customers with vision difficulties and customers without any vision problems, who are looking to purchase glasses that block off blue light from electronic devices or sunglasses. Our client is considering entering the overnight corrective contact lens market. They have asked our team to help them analyze whether they should enter the overnight corrective contact lens market.

Question 1: What are the key areas you would investigate to determine if they should enter the overnight corrective contact lens market?

Customers / market

- What is the TAM of the overnight corrective contact lens market? How is it growing? What is the profitability of this market?

- How are customer preferences trending in this eyewear space? Are customers trending away from glasses and towards contact lenses?

Competition

- Are there any competitors in the market? What does the competitor structure and market share look like (e.g., long tail of small competitors, monopoly, oligopoly)?

- What are the barriers to entry to entering this market?

Company

- Does our client have the capabilities to effectively enter and sell overnight corrective contact lenses?

- Would the distribution channels be similar to glasses?

- How would entering this contact lens market help the company achieve its goals?

If the decision is to go ahead with entering the overnight corrective contact lens market, there are three fundamental approaches:

- Build: build from scratch

- Buy: acquire an existing product or company

- Partner: partner with a company

Question 2: How big is the market for overnight corrective contact lenses?

- Size of market per year = volume of lenses sold per year x price per lens

- Volume of lenses sold per year:

  o Assume that this is limited to the U.S. currently for the initial launch

  o Number of people in the U.S. = 320 million

  o People who are within the appropriate age range to wear such lenses are 10 years old to 60 years old = (320 million / 80 years) x (60 years - 10 years) = 200 million

- Assume that percent of the population who need corrective eyewear is 50% = 200 million x 50% = 100 million

- Assume that percent of the population who wear contact lenses versus glasses is 30% = 100 million x 30% = 30 million

- Assume that the percent of people who would be interested in this type of lenses (overnight corrective contact lenses) is 20% of the contact lens wearing population = 30 million x 20% = 6 million

- Each wearer would usually need to purchase a contact lens for each eye = 6 million x 2 = 12 million

- Assume that these overnight corrective contact lenses need to be repurchased every two years = 12 million / 2 = 6 million per year

- Price per lens

  - Assume that there is only one existing SKU

  - A typical piece of disposable daily wear contact lens is $2 per lens

  - Since these overnight corrective contact lenses can be worn for a whole year, if they were to replace daily wear contact lenses, the estimated willingness to pay should be = $2 x 365 days = $730 or ~$700

  - There are potentially some added costs to these overnight lenses as you have to buy cleaning and storage solutions to repeat wear versus disposable daily contact lenses so we should discount the price for the overnight lenses. Assume that cleaning and storage solutions for a year probably cost about $100, therefore assume that the willingness to pay for the overnight lenses = ~$700 - $100 = ~$600

- Size of market per year = 12 million per year x $600 = $3.6B

Question 3: Let us say that the company decides to enter the overnight corrective lens market. However, in the first year, the CEO notices that this market segment is not performing as expected. Assume you are the Head of Sales. How would you go about improving sales?

- Lower pricing if this is a high price elasticity product

- Increase advertising that targets specific customer segments who would benefit most from such lenses (e.g., athletes, active lifestyle individuals, people with dry eyes who cannot wear normal lenses, etc.)

- Improve promotion and education among optometrists

- Increase the rate of changing to new lenses among consumers

- Increase number of SKUs to tackle more customer segments (e.g., overnight lenses with moisturizing capabilities)

- Increase sales commissions to encourage the sales team to make more sales

Question 4: The team finds that athletes and active individuals are the most likely to purchase such lenses and are huge promoters of these lenses once they have tried them. How would you target these customers?

- Start educating them in school and at workplaces

- Partner with sports teams and sports clubs to do in-person trainings and put up marketing materials

- Partner with a few influential athletes to be spokespersons for these lenses

- Carry out a case study to share how these lenses have improved the quality of life for such people and how these lenses can help the everyday person

- Partner and train optometrists to encourage them to recommend these lenses to customers

Question 5: The CEO calls you up one day and asks if you think the company should invest to enter this market. What would you say?

Yes, we believe that the company should enter the overnight corrective contact lens market because of a few reasons:

- Huge potential market size of $3.6B

- Market for such lenses is growing and very profitable

- Customers with vision difficulties have been preferring contact lenses over glasses due to convenience and comfort

- Few competitors in this market today

- The company already has infrastructure and distribution channels with optometrists, etc. in place to sell such lenses

However, there are risks involved with entering this new market and trade-offs as well:

- Achieving high sales depends greatly on a few "gatekeepers" such as optometrists encouraging adoption, and influential athletes, etc.

- Significant training and education needed as this is a relatively new product in the eyewear space compared to glasses, which are commonly understood

- Investing in these overnight contact lenses means trading off an opportunity to invest in another part of the business

We will need to continue doing additional research to create a 90-day plan for the launch and how to best ensure success.

Question 6: The CFO looks at your market sizing and questions your analysis. What would you do?

- First, I would offer to walk through the analysis and what the assumptions we made were and how we got to the final number

- Second, I would try to understand where we had different assumptions and drill deep into getting the most accurate numbers for those assumptions

- Third, for future meetings, I would share a pre-read with the senior team and offer to run through the numbers with the CFO prior to the executive meeting

Hotpot Co.

Problem statement

Our client is a hotpot manufacturer who produces mass-market hotpot devices with an average price of $100. Hotpot is a form of Asian cuisine and consists of adding raw ingredients into a boiling broth (kept warm on the dining table) to cook them. The actual hotpot device is a portable pot that boils the broth. They are interested in developing a premium hotpot product that will be priced at about $1,000. There are a couple of other players in the premium hotpot market. They have asked our team to help them estimate the size of the premium hotpot market and whether they should go ahead with developing this product or not.

Question 1: How would you estimate the size of the premium hotpot market?

- Assume that this product will be launched in the U.S. only initially

- It is unlikely that individuals in the same household would need their own hotpot device. It is more likely that each household will just have one hotpot device. Number of U.S. households = 100 million

- Assume that about 1% of U.S. households would be interested in purchasing a hotpot device = 100 million x 1% = 1 million

- Assume that only upper middle-class U.S. households would have the ability to purchase the premium hotpot product = 1 million x 20% = 0.2 million

- Assume that the premium hotpot product

will need to be replaced once every five years
= 0.2 million / 5 = 40,000 units per year

- Size of premium hotpot market per
  year = 40,000 x $1,000 = $40M

Question 2: Could this premium hotpot SKU achieve $100M in sales annually?

- Yes

  - If our client can capture a large share in the U.S. market *and* export the product internationally, our client might be able to achieve $100M in sales

- No

  - Since the estimated size of the premium hotpot market is $40M, this SKU cannot achieve $100M in sales annually if our client only sells within the U.S.

  - The premium hotpot market already has a few other large competitors who might have significant market share

  - Our client does not have the ability to manufacture and distribute enough premium hotpots in a year to achieve those skills

Question 3: After a year of launch, this premium hotpot SKU has not achieved the sales that we wanted. You are the Head of Sales. What would you do to improve sales?

- Explore direct to consumer sales

- Re-evaluate retail distribution partnerships

- Target certain B2B customer segments such as hotels, condominiums, restaurants, etc.

- Increase advertising that targets customer segments who can afford the premium line and around holiday seasons

- Increase the rate of changing out hotpot products to once every three years

- Increase sales commissions to encourage the sales team to make more sales

Question 4: Assume that the company has achieved a dominant share of the market for hotpot devices and is looking for new ways to increase revenues. What ideas would you explore?

- Sell additional related products such as BBQ grills, steamers, air fryers, etc.

- Sell accompanying products for hotpot devices such as hotpot mixes, sauces, etc.

- Increase prices for their hotpot devices since there are few to no substitutes in the market

- Sell their hotpot devices overseas

- Manufacture more SKUs of the hotpot devices (e.g., different colors, different styles such as retro, etc.)

Question 5: The CEO of the company has decided to leave his current role and start a separate company that is a spin-off of your last idea. He has asked you to join him. Would you take the

new job and what would you consider?

- Potential reasons for joining:

  - Learning and growth in the new job

  - Career aspirations

  - Passion for the idea

  - Working relationship with the CEO

- Not good reasons for joining:

  - Salary and compensation

  - Prestige of job

Question 6: At the executive meeting, you share your best ideas for generating new revenue. However, the executive team responds that they tried these ideas five years ago without success. What would you say to them?

- Understand why the ideas did not work five years ago

- Compare the differences five years ago and today

- Propose low-investment experiments to test out ideas today

Summer Storage

Problem statement

Our client is Mini Storage Co., an urban storage company that is based in the largest cities across the U.S. They are looking at expanding their offering to enter the summer storage market, specifically targeting students.

Our client has asked us to help them determine if they should enter the summer storage market and, if so, what they should do.

Question 1: How would you go about determining if the summer storage market is an attractive one?

Customers / market

- How big is the summer storage market?

- Is the summer storage market growing?

Competition

- Who are the competitors in the summer storage market?

- Has there been an increasing number of competitors in the market?

Product

- Would Mini Storage Co.'s product offering have to change to target summer storage? Would there need to be smaller storage offerings, etc.?

- What is the profitability of this offering / market?

Company

- Is Mini Storage Co. equipped to enter this market? Does it have the capabilities?

- How will marketing need to change to target this customer segment?

Question 2: How would you size the summer storage market?

- Size of market can be determined by number of storage units demanded per year x average price per storage unit per month x length of time units are used

- Number of storage units demanded per year:

    o Number of college students and graduate students in the geographical areas which are within a 50-mile radius of a Mini Storage Co. site

    o Percentage of students who would be interested in using a storage unit

- Average price per storage unit per month:

    o Willingness to pay is likely lower than a working adult or household who would use a storage unit

    o Compare against what competitors are pricing a similar storage unit at

    o Potentially need to price at 20% lower than market average

- Length of time units are used

o   Since the target audience typically has summer
for three months and would need such storage
for that corresponding amount of time

**Question 3: Assume that the company decided to
enter the summer storage market but has not seen the
expected amount of sales in the first year. You are the
Head of Sales. What would you do to improve sales?**

- Lower pricing to better meet this customer
segment's willingness to pay or run a short-
term marketing promotion

- Increase advertising that targets the student customer
segment by advertising in schools, around campuses, etc.

- Partner with schools to provide special packages
around storage and moving for their students

- Increase sales commissions to encourage
the sales team to make more sales

**Question 4: The company is currently only able to
cater to urban schools due to the location of their
storage facilities today. The company is looking to
invest in warehouses that are within 20 miles of some
large universities. What would you consider when
deciding whether to invest in these warehouses?**

- ROI of investment - how much would it cost for the
company to rent these warehouses compared to how
much the company can rent out these storage units for

- Outside of summer storage, would these storage
units sit empty or would there be additional

business from surrounding neighborhoods

- What are other competitive options for the nearby universities (i.e., if there is a storage facility within 10 miles, why would students drive out to this further warehouse)

Question 5: The CEO of Mini Storage Co. asks for an update on your findings to date. What would you say?

We believe that the summer storage market is not advisable to enter into given the relatively small size, only relevant for 3 months of the year, and the presumed low willingness of students to pay given their limited disposable income. Additionally, given the location of our urban facilities today, the company pays relatively high real estate costs and will need to charge higher prices to rent out these storage units.

We will need additional data on the price that students are willing to pay for those summer months and compare that to the price that we need to charge to hit our ROI goals. We will also need to understand this opportunity relative to other opportunities in order to prioritize where and how we should spend our resources. For example, given our urban locations, we might want to target upmarket consumers.

San Francisco Ballet Company

Problem statement

Our client is the San Francisco Ballet Company, a non-profit ballet performance group based in San Francisco city. The ballet company is a well-known performing arts company and regularly performs not just in the U.S. but also internationally. However, in the last five years, the San Francisco Ballet Company has seen its revenue stall.

Our client's revenues come from primarily two sources. The first is earned revenue in the form of ticket revenue and yearly subscriptions to performances. The second is donations by individuals, companies, government organizations, and charities. Our client has asked us to help identify areas to grow its revenue over the next 5 years.

Question 1: How would you calculate the company's revenue?

- Revenue sources are earned revenue and donations:

- Earned revenue:

  o Ticket revenue = number of consumers x number of tickets sold per consumer x average price of ticket

  o Yearly subscriptions to performance = number of subscribers x average cost of yearly subscription

  o Merchandise revenue = volume of merchandise sold x average price per unit of merchandise

- Donations:

  o Regular donors = number of donors x amount

donated per donor on yearly basis

- o Special donation events (e.g., charity galas) = number of events per year x average amount donated per event

Question 2: Earned revenue has historically been the company's largest revenue stream. However, earned revenue has decreased significantly in the past 5 years. What recommendations would you share to turn this around?

- Increase ticket prices and/or take advantage of price discrimination opportunities

- Increase the number of performances each year, particularly during holiday seasons

- Change the performance mix to cater to changing consumer demand (e.g., if consumers are preferring more contemporary ballet performances)

- Increase sales and marketing to target consumers who are interested in the ballet and with willingness to pay

- Target new customer segments that might be showing interest in the ballet (e.g., younger generation, college students)

Question 3: Your team gets sales and market data from the company. You find that ticket and subscription pricing has stayed the same over the past decade. What conclusions can you draw from these data and what might be the drivers behind these results?

Revenue ($M)	5 years ago	4 years ago	3 years ago	2 years ago	Last year

Single ticket sales	1.5	1.7	1.9	2.2	2.4
Quarterly season subscription sales	3.1	3.0	2.9	2.8	2.7
Annual subscription sales	3.5	3.4	3.4	2.8	2.2
Percentage of sub-scribers who renewed	*85%*	*80%*	*74%*	*72%*	*71%*
Merchandise sales	0.2	0.3	0.5	0.4	0.4

Conclusions:

- Earned income is decreasing because of a decline in subscription sales

- Single ticket sales and merchandise sales have been increasing; however, these do not fully offset the decline in subscription sales

- Subscriber renewal rates have been decreasing over time as well, which likely partially accounts for the declining subscription sales

Possible drivers behind these results:

- Subscribers may be migrating to shorter commitment options. The significant decline in annual subscriptions, smaller decline in quarterly subscriptions, and increase in single ticket revenue suggest that customers are shifting away from up-front, higher-commitment purchases

- The rate of adding new subscribers has declined substantially. This could also be associated with new customers preferring low-commitment purchases

- Economy could be undergoing a recession. Going to the ballet is considered a non-essential need (at least for most people) and with a recession and lower disposable income, more consumers could have reduced their consumption in this area

- Competing options for entertainment. There could be increasing number of substitutions such as more musicals, plays, and other performing art options

- Shrinking customer segment due to age (e.g., historically ballet goers were older, high-income people)

- Shift in customer preferences to other options of entertainment. Ballet goers might have a change in preference to going to other live performance options (e.g., classical music concerts, pop music concerts, etc.)

Question 4: Your client believes that subscribers tend to have a high lifetime value over an average lifespan of 3 years. They have asked your team to calculate the average lifetime value of a new subscriber. The client has the following historical data on subscribers:

- Average revenue from a subscriber in Year 1 = $300

- Average revenue from a subscriber in Year 2 = $500

- Total average annual revenue for a subscriber from Year 3 onwards = $1,000

- Number of new subscribers last year = 2,200 (not needed for calculation)

- Number of new subscribers two years ago = 1,200 (not needed for calculation)

Only provided if candidate asks for it:

- Renewal rate after Year 1 = 80%

- Renewal rate after Year 2 = 50%

- Renewal rates for Years 3+ = 20%

Expected revenue per subscriber in Year 1 = $300

Expected revenue per subscriber in Year 2 = $500 x 80% = $400

Expected revenue per subscriber for Year 3 = $1,000 x 80% x 50% = $400

Expected lifetime revenue per subscriber = ($300 + $400 + $400) = $1,100

Question 5: Your team finds that other performing arts organizations have customers with an average lifetime value of $1,500. How much would our client's average revenue per subscriber in year 2 need to increase to get a total expected lifetime value of $1,500?

Assume renewal rates do not change.

Assume X = new average revenue in year 2

Expected lifetime revenue per subscriber = 300 + (X x 80%) + $400 = $1,500

X = $800 / 80% = $1,000

Average revenue per subscriber in year 2 would need to increase by: $1,000 / $500 -1 = 200% - 1 = 100%

Question 6: The CEO of the San Francisco Ballet Company would also like to look into how their donation

amounts are performing. How would you assess how the company is doing with donations received?

- Benchmark based on the industry and how peers are doing:

  o Amount of donations received

  o Breakdown of donation sources

- Top down analysis

  o Size of performing arts market and associated donation pool

  o SFBC's share of the donor pool

- Historical trends

  o Historical amount of donations received in absolute numbers

  o Percentage of donations received by city relative to wealth concentrated by city, etc.

  o Percentage of donations received by level of household income relative to wealth concentrated in those household demographics

Question 7: The CEO of the San Francisco Ballet Company meets with the team and asks you for a synthesis of recommendations for how they could turn things around. What would you say?

We determined that earned income is decreasing because of a decline in subscription sales. Single ticket sales and merchandise sales have been increasing; however, these do not fully offset the decline in subscription sales. Subscriber renewal rates have been decreasing over time as well, which likely partially accounts for the declining subscription sales.

The main drivers behind these results were:

- Subscribers migrating to shorter commitment options

- The rate of adding new subscribers has declined substantially

- There is an increasing number of competing options for entertainment. There could be increasing number of substitutions such as more musicals, plays, and other performing art options

- Shrinking customer segment due to age (e.g., historically ballet goers were older, high-income people)

As such, we would recommend a few actions:

- Improve subscriber renewal rates (especially first-year subscribers). Focused market research efforts to understand why new subscribers are not renewing should be undertaken, and appropriate adjustments (product, advertising, channel, pricing) should be made

- Adjust the pricing to be more in line with market rates and price discriminate based on performance type and target customer segment

- Explore ways to cost effectively increase the number of new subscribers. Given that their audience is aging, finding ways to appeal new and younger customer segments to continue growing their customer population

- Adjust advertising to target single ticket consumers in a bid to improve this revenue stream (e.g., how do they hear about performances, what are their needs)

- Increase the number of charitable events to improve donations. Appoint influential current customers who are willing to lend their influence to carry out charitable events

However, with pursuing these recommendations, we would need to be cognizant of some potential risks:

- Potential for cannibalization of subscriptions by encouraging single ticket sales

- Lack of sales and marketing expertise in the organization to carry out such recommendations

- Tradeoff of pursuing these recommendations that would consumer financial resources, attention, and time that could be spent on other pursuits

Tigerfence

Problem statement

Our client is a media company called Tigerfence that used to focus on the production of TV shows. They are considering entering the online TV streaming industry, similar to Netflix and Amazon Prime. They have approached us to ask for help determining if they should enter the online TV streaming industry.

Question 1: What would you look into in order to determine whether this online TV streaming service is a good idea?

Customers / market:

- Size of market for online TV streaming (both within U.S. and internationally)

- Customer demand and growth trends for the market

Product:

- Price of online TV streaming services

- ROI of the service

- Product differentiation compared to competitors in the market

- Opportunities to sell synergistic products along with online TV streaming (e.g., ads)

Competitors:

- Number of competitors in the direct market (e.g., competitors in the online TV streaming space) and related spaces (e.g., conventional TV services)

Company:

- Capabilities of company to enter this market

Question 2: What would you do to try to determine the potential revenue that could be made from this idea per year?

- Potential revenue per year = volume of online TV streaming services sold annually x average price for each streaming subscription per year + other forms of revenue

- Volume of online TV streaming services:

  o Assumption is each household will only purchase one such online TV streaming service

  o Internet penetration in the U.S. among households

  o Percentage of the population that watches TV, split by frequency of TV watching

  o Percentage of internet users in each frequency category who would be interested in online TV streaming services

- Average price for each streaming subscription per year

  o Competitors' pricing as a benchmark

  o Consumer willingness to pay

  o Cost-based pricing to understand what the price needs to be to achieve target gross margins

- Other forms of revenue

     ○   Potential revenue opportunity from selling paid ads

Question 3: How would you go about sizing the market opportunity of online TV streaming services alone? You can ignore the other forms of revenue.

- Assume market opportunity is mainly in the U.S. initially

- Number of households in the U.S. = 100 million

- Assume 70% of households in the U.S. have internet access = 70 million households

- Assume 60% of households with internet access watch some TV = 70 million x 60% = 42 million

- Assume that the TV-watching population can be split into two categories evenly:

  - Frequent TV watchers, who have higher willingness to pay for additional features, such as early access to the newest TV shows, no paid ads during viewing, etc. = 42 million x 50% = 21 million

  - Moderate TV watchers, who have a lower willingness to pay for "premium" features = 42 million x 50% = 21 million

- Assume that the TV subscription price is differentiated into two main SKUs:

  - Premium SKU (includes no ads, early access to the newest TV shows) = $30 per month

  - Standard SKU (includes some paid ads, delayed access to newest TV shows) = $10 per month

- Of frequent TV watchers, assume that approximately 33% of them would be interested in purchasing online TV streaming services = 21 million / 3 = 7 million

- Of moderate TV watchers, assume that approximately 10% would be interested in purchasing online TV streaming services = 21 million / 10 = 2.1 million

- Total market size of online TV streaming service = (7 million x 30 x 12) + (2.1 million x 10 x 12) = 2,520 million + 252 million = $2,772 million or ~$3B

Question 4: The team compiled some data on the major online TV streaming services today. What can you conclude from the data and what do you think is driving these results?

	Year 1	Year 2	Year 3	Year 4	Year 5
Total number of subscribers	12m	18m	36m	49m	65m
Total revenue	$470m	$570m	$860m	$1030m	$1120m
Total paid advertising	$86m	$104m	$135m	$172m	$211m

- The total number of subscribers has been increasing each year for the past five years. This means overall demand for online TV streaming services has been increasing, which suggests that the market is growing, and customers are moving towards this form of TV

- Total revenue has also been increasing correspondingly each year, but the rate of increase has been lower than the total number of subscribers. This suggests that the price of the service has been decreasing year over year, potentially due to an increasing number of competitors and other pricing pressures

- Total paid advertising revenue is higher than the online TV streaming revenue, suggesting that it is a very profitable source of revenue and could help to "subsidize" additional investments in building the attractiveness of online TV streaming to consumers

- Total paid advertising revenue is also increasing year over year, suggesting that more and more companies are viewing online TV streaming as an increasingly attractive marketing channel, likely due to the large and growing customer base, and income level of consumers

Question 5: The CEO of Tigerfence asks you to share your findings. What would you say?

Based on our findings, we would recommend entering the online TV streaming service for a few reasons:

- The size of market for online TV streaming (both within U.S. and internationally) is large and growing quickly

- Opportunities to sell synergistic products along with online TV streaming (e.g., ads) is high

However, Tigerfence will need to still invest a significant amount of resources and marketing dollars to convert more conventional TV-watching customers to its service in order to take share away from its offline competitors.

Pricing

T-Phone Co.

Problem statement

Our client is a large electronics company that has produced popular laptops and computer accessories. They have recently decided to enter the smartphone market as they believe that smartphones could replace the need for laptops in the future. They have developed a flip smartphone, which has all the functions that an iPhone or Google Pixel has. They have asked our team to help them with pricing their smartphone to sell into the global market.

Question 1: What are the key areas you would look into for pricing this smartphone?

With any product, there are three ways to price it:

- Cost-based pricing:

    ○ What are the goals of T-Phone Co. in the short-term and long-term (e.g., do they want to aggressively gain market share or which would suggest pricing lower or are they interested in market positioning or profits and might price a little higher)?

    ○ What would it cost T-Phone Co. to manufacture, distribute, and market this phone?

    ○ What is the breakeven point and what is the profit margin T-Phone Co. wants to earn on this product?

- Competitor-based pricing:

- How are competitors' products priced (in T-Phone's case, how do competitors like Apple and Google price their phone)

- How does this product compare to competitors' products / how differentiated is the product? Are there any substitutions?

- What will the competitive response be?

• Price-based costing:

- What are consumers willing to pay for this product? (e.g., are they willing to pay a premium for the flip functionality, vs. the "candy bar" style phones from Apple and Google?)

- At consumers' willingness to pay prices, will the company be able to make the profit margin that they want?

- What is this product worth to consumers? What are they currently paying for similar substitutes?

Question 2: Although T-Phone Co. has been an electronics producer for a while, this is the first smartphone they have produced. Which pricing strategy would you suggest that they implement?

From what I understand, the market for smartphones is very competitive. There are many high-quality and highly marketed and branded options already (e.g., iPhone, Pixel, Samsung Galaxy, etc.) The companies have also spent a great deal of resources on marketing and branding their products. As such, it is difficult to implement cost-based pricing since this price might not resonate with customers, and it would be difficult to compete with the big companies in this space as well.

Along the same lines, competitor-based pricing is also difficult for T-Phone Co. As mentioned in the problem statement, even if T-Phone's smartphone is very comparable to an iPhone or Pixel and has all of the best features, the customer recognition and willingness to pay could be very different for an iPhone vs. T-Phone's smartphone. This is a likely scenario given the years that competitors have spent marketing their products.

As such, I would recommend that T-Phone Co. apply a price-based costing approach. What would consumers be willing to pay for T-Phone Co.'s smartphone? What is this product worth to consumers and what are they paying for similar substitutes (e.g., new smartphones that, similarly, do not have a large marketing brand, etc.)?

Lino Italian Restaurant

Problem statement

Our client is a restaurant called Lino that sells Italian food and is well known for their pasta. They have recently developed a new lasagna dish made with truffles and aged cheese. They have asked you to help them with pricing this new lasagna dish.

Question 1: What are the key areas you would look into for pricing this smartphone?

With any product, there are three ways to price it:

- Cost-based pricing:

    o   What does it cost Lino to produce this lasagna dish? How much is the all-in cost for ingredients, labor costs, etc.?

    o   What is the breakeven point and what is the profit margin Lino wants to earn on this dish?

- Competitor-based pricing:

    o   How are competitors' lasagna dishes priced?

    o   How does this lasagna compare to competitors' lasagna? How differentiated is it? Do they also use relatively expensive ingredients like truffle and aged cheese?

    o   What is the price of substitute dishes such as regular Italian pasta or pizza?

- Price-based costing:

○ What are consumers willing to pay for this dish? Would a consumer be willing to pay a much higher price than regular lasagna because of the quality of ingredients included, or the 'hype" associated with truffle-infused dishes in recent years?

○ At consumers' willingness to pay prices, will Lino be able to make the profit margin that they want?

○ What are consumers currently paying for similar substitutes?

Mergers And Acquisitions

Bark Universe

Problem statement

Our client is an investment firm looking to acquire Bark Universe, a chain of dog food & dog product stores. Bark Universe owns and operates 500 stores across the U.S. and another 500 stores internationally. All the stores are located in shopping complexes. Bark Universe sells a wide range of dog products, such as dog kibble, fresh dog food, dog leashes, collars, dog toys, grooming tools, and more to consumers. A select number of stores also offer dog grooming and dog hotel services.

Our client has asked you to analyze the industry and provide a recommendation on whether they should acquire Bark Universe or not.

Question 1: What issues do you think the team should look into when considering whether our client should buy this company?

Since this is an investment firm, the main considerations will be around whether there is potential to grow the value of Bark Universe further and exit (i.e., sell the company) for a good profit. As such, we should look into:

- Market:

    o What is the TAM of this dog product market?

    o How is the market growing? Are specific product categories growing faster or slower than others?

- o   What is the profitability of this market? By product?

- o   What does the competitor landscape look like?

- o   Are there high barriers to entry for new competitors?

- Financials:

  - o   What is the availability of capital to buy Bark Universe?

  - o   What is the potential to increase revenue and profit margins for Bark Universe?

  - o   What does cash flow look like at Bark Universe? Are there clear ways to increase cash flow?

  - o   Based on historicals, how do we expect financials to trend in 5 years' time? What does the exit value and potential look like?

- Growth:

  - o   Are there clear ways to improve growth quickly? Can we double down on product categories that are high profit margin?

  - o   Can we sell off areas of the business which are low profit margin or negative profit margin?

Question 2: What do you think are the drivers of growth in the dog product market?

The drivers of growth vary by product category. Dog hotel services will be driven by different specific factors than dog grooming products, for example. However, some categories of drivers that can be applicable across categories are:

- Customer population trends:

    o More people are adopting or purchasing dogs as pets year over year

    o Customer change in preferences (e.g., for more specialized dog diets that include probiotics)

    o Customer change in distribution channel preferences (e.g., buying things online, esp. impulse purchases)

    o Fads such as grooming one's dog in a specific manner, potentially driven by certain influencer dogs

    o Increasing willingness to spend on dog care

- Competitor trends:

    o More competitors by product category, which can hinder growth

    o More widespread distribution of products from specialized dog stores to common availability in grocery stores

    o Increased marketing from competitors around dog care

    o Additional online competitors (e.g., Chewy.com)

- Product:

    o New dog product innovations that lead to better dog products

    o Wider diversity of dog products (e.g.,

more color SKUs, more designs)

- Economy:

    o   Economic climate determines disposable income and willingness to spend (e.g., lower willingness to spend in a recession)

Question 3: The team estimates that half of dog owners send their dogs for regular grooming sessions. The average grooming session costs $100. What would be the impact on gross profit if 50% more dog owners sent their dogs for regular grooming sessions?

Current gross profit = number of dog grooming sessions per year x gross profit per grooming session

- Assume gross profit per grooming session is 50% of total revenue = $100 x 50% = $50

- Number of dog grooming sessions per year:

    o   Number of households in the U.S. = 100 million

    o   Assume 20% of households have dogs = 100 million x 20% = 20 million

    o   Assume that a quarter of these households have two dogs = (20 million / 4) * 2 = 10 million dogs

    o   Total number of dogs as pets in the U.S. = (20 million x ¾) + 10 million = 25 million dogs

    o   Assume that half of households send their dogs for regular grooming sessions while the remaining half groom their dogs by themselves = 25 million / 2 = 12.5 million

- o Assume that groomed dogs receive an average grooming of once per month = 12.5 million x 12 months = 150 million grooming session a year

- Gross profit per year currently = 150 million x $50 = $7,500 million

New gross profit per year:

- If 50% more dog owners sent their dogs for grooming sessions = 150 million / 2 = 75 million grooming sessions

- Additional gross profit = 75 million x $50 = $3,750 million

Of course, the average number of grooming sessions depends on the breed of dog, the environment where the dog lives in (e.g., a hotter climate might cause a dog to require more frequent grooming), economic climate, etc.

Question 4: In order to justify the cost of the acquisition, the team has determined that profit margins must be at least 70%. Margins are currently 50%. What would you recommend for Bark Universe to increase margins?

Profits = Revenue - Costs

In order to increase profit margins, you can either increase revenue or decrease cost or do both.

Strategies to increase revenue:

- Raise prices on selected price inelastic products and/or services

- Promote sales of higher profit margin

products through more marketing

- Change mix of product offering to focus on higher profit margin products and discontinue low profit margin products

- Open new stores in high-foot traffic areas or geographic locations with significant dog density

- Start an online presence for Bark Universe to increase sales among the online consumer segment

Strategies to decrease cost:

- Shut down stores that are cash flow and profit margin negative

- Negotiate with suppliers to reduce the cost of goods sold

- Improve operational efficiency of delivery and distribution to reduce costs

- Reduce costs of salaries of employees by negotiating with labor unions

- Renegotiate real estate leases to reduce rent paid for stores

Question 5: Our client has seen some large retailers like Safeway increase its offering of dog products recently. They are concerned that such retailers would push out specialty stores like Bark Universe. Do you think this will happen?

Yes, this will likely happen because:

- Large retailers can offer significantly lower prices than specialty stores. This would potentially cause some cost-conscious consumers to switch away from specialty stores

- Large retailers offer a wider variety of products beyond just dog products, and can offer convenience for shoppers who want to get all their household goods at one shop

- Large retailers are usually located in very convenient locations for shoppers

No, this is unlikely to happen because:

- Specialty store customers are not very price sensitive and are willing to spend significant amounts to provide their dog with the best care

- Large retailers are unlikely to carry more unique products versus specialty stores that will have a wider selection of products, and the latest new dog products

- Specialty stores are likely to have better customer service teams who are trained and knowledgeable about dog care

Question 6: Your client has called for a steering committee meeting to discuss your team's findings. What would you tell your client?

Based on our findings, we would recommend that you acquire Bark Universe for a few major reasons:

- Large and growing market, and increasing willingness to spend on dog care suggests a fundamentally attractive market

- Few competitors in the dog product market that are similar in size and breadth as Bark Universe

- Perceived limited threat from large retailers

However, profit margins are currently lower than desired at 50%. We would need to aggressively implement strategies to either increase revenue or decrease costs. Ideally, we would be able to do both.

Some short-term strategies to increase revenue are:

- Raise prices on selected price inelastic products and/or services

- Change mix of product offering to focus on higher profit margin products and discontinue low profit margin products

Some short-term strategies to decrease cost:

- Shut down stores that are cash flow and profit margin negative

- Reduce costs of salaries of employees by negotiating with labor unions

However, we would need to be careful of threats by large retailers and a growing number of specialty competitors. Of course, the acquisition would also need to depend on the asking price for Bark Universe and additional diligence on customer satisfaction, repeat customer purchases, etc. We will also need to consider if the company has a talented management team who would be able to drive the suggested changes going forward.

Frozen Treasures

Problem statement

Our client is Frozen Treasures (FT), an ice cream chain that competes with Haagen Daz, Ben & Jerry's, Coldstone Creamery, and more. FT is the third largest ice cream chain worldwide based on its yearly revenues. Similar to most of its competitors, FT offers ice cream for onsite consumption (e.g., cup or cone orders), and takeaway orders (e.g., pint or bucket orders).

FT owns some of the stores in its chain and franchises the rest of the stores, which make up approximately 80% of all FT stores. The franchisees pay FT a franchise fee and take direction on major business decisions, such as the menu, store theme, etc. from FT's head office.

FT's Growth team has suggested acquisition as an attractive strategy to grow quickly in the next five years. One of the top acquisition targets is Healthy Waffles (HW), a waffle producer with factories in the U.S., Europe, and Asia and stores globally. HW produces both conventional waffles made from regular wheat flour and "healthier" waffle options made using buckwheat flour, rice flour, and almond flour. Unlike FT, HW owns all of its stores and does not have any franchises.

FT has reached out to our team to help them determine if FT should acquire HW.

Question 1: What are the key areas you would look into to determine whether FT should acquire HW?

- Company: are there efficiencies from combining operations (e.g., G&A, S&M), are there risks to cultural integration, are there efficiencies from combining distribution channels, are there tax advantages, how will shareholder value improve, are there synergies or risks from combining the management talent, has FT done an acquisition before and are there acquisition challenges, what is the capital needed to fund this acquisition

- Products: will this diversify the product catalogue and/or cannibalize existing products, are the products from both companies compatible and synergistic (i.e., does one product fit a need that the other product requires), are there any R&D synergies or risks, what is the profitability of HW's waffle products

- Market: will this M&A increase market share in a particular industry, how big is the waffle market, is the waffle market growing and projected to grow, how will competitors in both ice cream and waffle markets respond, are there any legal or regulatory risks to the M&A

Question 2: The client shared the following data on FT and HW. What do you think are potential synergies from acquiring HW?

Stores	FT	HW
North America	2,000	1,000
South America	300	280
Europe	1,400	600
Asia	1,200	800
Total	4,900	2,680
No. of stores newly opened each year	20	50

Financials	FT	HW
Total sales	$1,600M	$700M
Average sales per store	$327K	$260K
Key expenses (as % of sales)		
Cost of goods sold	45%	40%
Store operating expenses	20%	24%
G&A expenses	7%	16%
Sales & marketing expenses	8%	12%

There are potential synergies for both revenue gains and cost savings.

For revenue gain:

- Sell HW goods in FT stores and vice versa (selling FT goods in HW stores)

- FT could share learnings on managing store operating expenses with HW to reduce HW's store operating expenses

- FT could share sales strategy for how to improve store sales with HW (FT is currently making almost double the amount of sales per store as HW)

For cost savings:

- Combine S&M marketing efforts for FT and HW

- Combine G&A departments (e.g., accounting, billing, etc.)

- Negotiate better costs for raw materials (e.g., milk, eggs) with suppliers since the combined company would be purchasing a larger volume

Question 3: The team thinks that the synergies from the combined FT and HW company should be able to double FT's U.S. market share in the next five years. Considering only FT stores, what will be the average sales per FT store in order to double FT's U.S. market share?

- First, you need the U.S. market size for ice cream:

  - Assume that ice cream consumption per individual in the U.S. that consumes ice cream is, on average, $10 per month, and is expected to stay approximately the same over the next 5 years

  - Size of U.S. population = 320 million

  - Assume that approximately 60% of the U.S. population consumes ice cream = 320 million x 60% = ~180 million

  - Expected U.S. market size = ~180 million x $10 x 12 months = $21 billion

- Second, FT's current U.S. market share = $1.6B / $21B = 7.6%

  - Doubling FT's market share in five years

$$= \$21B \times (7.6\% \times 2) = \$3.2B$$

- Third, number of FT stores in five years
  = (20 x 5) + 4,900 = 5,000 stores

- Lastly, average sales per FT store = \$3.2B / 5,000 = \$640K

  - % increase in sales = \$640 / \$327 = ~2x or double

This seems like a realistic growth target since the addition of HW products to FT stores would increase sales, and FT could also increase the variety of its products and flavors to appeal to more consumers.

Question 4: One of the synergies mentioned earlier is the idea of selling FT products in HW stores and vice versa. How would you determine the impact of this approach on profitability for the stores?

Profits = Revenue - Costs

- Incremental revenue:

  - What are the incremental sales / revenues we would get from selling FT products in HW stores and vice versa (price x volume sold)

  - Will there be any cannibalization of sales if consumers view waffles and ice cream as substitutes for each other

- Incremental costs:

  - What are the incremental variable costs from having to produce and sell these goods (additional training for staff to make the goods, additional distribution channels to ensure that ingredients get to these new stores, etc.)

○   What are the incremental fixed costs from having to sell these goods (e.g., more kitchen space per store needed for additional equipment to manufacture ice cream or waffles, etc.)

Question 6: The CEO of FT calls for a meeting and asks for an update on the team's findings so far. What would you say on whether FT should acquire HW or not?

Our findings suggest that acquiring HW would lead to significant value for FT, and FT should acquire HW for a couple of reasons:

- The synergies of the combined entity would enable higher profits from being able to both achieve revenue gain and cost savings

- Waffle consumption is growing in the U.S. and internationally, and HW is also one of the earlier pioneers in healthy dessert eating, which FT could benefit from.

- HW's target consumer segments are also different from FT and tend to be the more health-conscious consumer or nutritious-focused parent. Together, FT and HW could target additional consumer segments to expand their customer base

Through some initial sizing, we believe that acquiring HW could double the average sales per FT store in the next five years from selling HW products in FT stores and also sharing some of the learnings and efforts around sales and marketing.

However, the decision on whether to acquire or not is also highly dependent on acquisition cost for HW as well as the company's other priorities.

Other "Non-Archetypical" Cases

Organic Winery

Problem statement

Your client is a businesswoman who is looking to start her own winery in upstate New York. She currently lives in New York City and works in a corporate role, but has always dreamed of starting her own winery that produces organic wines

Renting a plot of land in upstate New York for a year will require about a quarter of a million dollars. She has asked you if she should embark on this new venture.

Question 1: What areas would you investigate to determine if this is a good idea or not?

- Customers / market

  o How big is the market opportunity for organic wines?

  o What are the growth trends of this market?

  o Who are potential customers and is that population increasing?

- Company

  o What kind of employees or experience will she need and who will be a part of the team?

  o Aside from the $500,000 to start the venture, what other financing is needed and how long can the $500,000 last in running the business?

- o What is the amount of production and sales needed over a period of time to start breaking even with costs?

- **Product**

  - o Are there barriers to starting this venture? (e.g., licenses needed for winery, certification for organic wine)

  - o How will this product be launched in the market?

  - o What kind of marketing is needed around organic wine?

  - o What are the distribution channels required for wine?

  - o Can this wine be exported internationally or shipped to further away states domestically or will it go bad if stored for too long?

  - o How is this wine differentiated from existing wine options in the market?

  - o Would the taste of organic wine appeal to consumers?

- **Competition**

  - o Are there competitors in this market?

  - o Is the competition consolidated or fragment?

Question 2: What is the size of the domestic organic wine market in the U.S.?

- Product will be launched in the U.S.

- Size of organic wine market per year = number of wine bottles sold per year x price per bottle

- Size of U.S. population = 320 million

- Average life expectancy of U.S. person = 80 years

- Assume average number of glasses of wine per bottle = 6 glasses

- Number of people who can drink wine in the U.S. have to be above age 21 = (320 / 80) x (80 - 21) = ~240 million

- Assume total number of people who drink wine in the U.S. is 40% = 240 million x 40% = ~100 million

- Assume that there are three categories of wine drinkers, and the group of wine drinkers is split evenly among the three categories:

  - Light drinkers who drink an average of one glass of wine every month = (100 million / 3) * (12 months * 1 glass / month * (1 bottle / 6 glasses)) = ~66 million bottles of wine per year

  - Moderate drinkers who drink an average of one bottle of wine every month = (100 million / 3) x (12 months * 1 bottle / month) = 400 million bottles of wine per year

  - Heavy drinkers who drink an average of one bottle of wine each week = (100 million / 3) x (12 months * 4 bottles / month) = 1600 million bottles of wine per year

- Total number of bottles of wine consumed each year = ~2060 million bottles of wine per year

- Assume that 5% of the wine-drinker population care about the benefits of organic wine, and would purchase organic wine

- Assume that the average price for a bottle of organic wine is $15

- Total size of organic wine market = ~2,000 million * 5% * $15 = ~$150 million

Question 3: After seeing the total market opportunity, your client decides that this is likely a good venture. However, she is concerned about the upfront investment costs. What are some of the upfront investment costs that she will need to consider?

- Major upfront costs:

  o Land rent or purchase

  o Equipment to plant grapes and equipment to harvest and process grapes into wine

  o Grape costs to start planting

  o Irrigation costs

  o Other material costs such as stakes in the group, wiring, etc.

  o Utilities

- Other potential costs are:

- Licensing

- Taxes

- Vehicles

- Refrigeration equipment

Question 4: You determine that the total costs for the first year of operations are going to be approximately $500,000. If your client is planning on selling each bottle of wine for $10, how many bottles of wine must your client sell in the first year to break even?

- Total costs = $500,000

- Assume that the number of bottles of wine that your client must sell is Y

- Average gross profit at breakeven point = $0

- Therefore, $0 = Revenue - Costs of the first year = ($10 x Y) - $500,000

  - $500,000 = $10 x Y

  - Y = 50,000 bottles of wine

Question 5: Your client tells you that she thinks the winery will be able to produce 50,000 bottles of wine, if producing at 100% efficiency, in its second year, and the winery will be at 60% efficiency only in the first year. How long will it take for your client to break even?

- Breakeven point:

164

- o Total costs over period of time = Total revenue over period of time

- Total costs over period of time:

  - o Total costs for first year of operations = $500,000

  - o Assume that total costs for second year of operations are 50% of first year since you do not need to repurchase capital-intensive equipment and grape vines, etc. = $500,000 x 50% = $250,000

- Total revenue over period of time:

  - o Assuming even distribution of bottle production, number of bottles of wine produced in first year = 50,000 x 60% = 30,000 bottles

  - o Assuming even distribution of bottle production, number of bottles of wine produced in second year = 50,000 bottles

- Breakeven point:

  - o Assume that Z is the number of months of year 2

  - o $500,000 + ($250,000 x Z/12) = (30,000 + (50,000 x Z/12)) x $10

  - o 50,000 + 25,000 x Z/12 = 30,000 + (50,000 x Z/12)

  - o 20,000 + 25,000 x Z/12 = 50,000 x Z/12

  - o 20,000 = 25,000 x Z/12

  - o Z = (4 / 5) x 12 = ~10 months in year 2

  - o It will take 12 months in year 1 + 10 months

in year 2 = 22 months to break even

Question 6: Your client calls you up and asks whether this seems like a good venture given your findings in this case. What would you say to her?

Although the market opportunity for organic wine is large, given the high upfront investment required, I would recommend ensuring that you have sufficient financial capital to finance this venture for at least two years as well as the right talent and experience to pursue this, as producing organic wine requires specialized knowledge.

There are also certain risks to this business such as weather changes, seasonal variances in cash flow (peaks around holiday seasons), sensitivity to pest infections, regulation around alcohol, etc. which you will need to consider as well.

That being said, there is more to pursuing a business venture than just the ROI. If you are passionate about wine production and this venture would help you to fulfill your personal and professional goals, then this is another important factor to include in your decision-making equation.

Latex Manufacturing

Problem statement

Our client is a U.K. manufacturer of latex goods that are sold to retailers. The company has many product lines, but their main product lines are: (1) gloves and (2) latex beds. They produce 300,000kg of latex goods annually today. However, consumers are demanding more goods and there is currently a delay in production in the U.K. The CEO believes that if they could produce even more goods, there would be more than enough demand to purchase them.

The CEO has been concerned about the increasingly high cost of production in the U.K. due to the strength of unions in the U.K. She is wondering if the company should offshore their production to a lower-cost country like India, China, or Vietnam. She believes that they would be able to increase production by 33% in an offshore location as well. She has asked our team to help her determine whether they should offshore their production.

Question 1: What are the key areas you would look into to determine if our client should offshore to a lower-cost country?

- Pros

  - Cost savings: What are the main cost savings our client can derive from offshoring? The main benefit would be lower production costs, mostly driven from likely lower labor costs, lower land costs, etc. However, this has to be weighed against potentially higher distribution and delivery costs to send the produced goods to the U.K. or retailers' locations from the offshored location. Labor cost savings also need to be tempered against potentially lower labor productivity, which would cut into the savings.

- o   Revenue gains: Would starting an offshore location in Asia allow our client to build a network for selling their goods in the Asian market? The closer proximity, lower cost of goods produced, and presence in Asia could allow our client to enter a new geographical market, thereby increasing sales.

- Cons / Risks

  - o   Quality of goods: Are there potential quality issues with the production of latex goods? Offshoring production could lead to lower quality issues, potentially longer manufacturing times, etc. This could affect sales and lower customer satisfaction, etc.

  - o   Management issues: What is the medium for communication in these countries? Could there be potential for communication or coordination issues?

Question 2: The team consolidates a set of data on production. How much could our client save by offshoring to India?

Cost categories	Costs in U.K. (per kg)	Costs in India relative to U.K.
Labor	£0.50	30%
Equipment maintenance	£0.10	50%
Raw materials	£0.30	66%
Transportation	£0.20	200%

Total		

- Costs per kg:

  - Total costs per kg in the U.K. = £0.50 + £0.10 + £0.30 + £0.20 = £1.10

  - Total costs per kg in India = (£0.50 x 30%) + (£0.10 x 50%) + (£0.30 x 66%) + (£0.20 x 200%) = £0.80

- Volume produced:

  - Current volume produced in the U.K. = 3,000,000kg (given in initial problem statement)

  - Expected volume produced in India = 3,000,000kg x 133% = 4,000,000kg (given in initial problem statement)

- Total cost savings from offshoring = total costs in the U.K. - total costs in India

  - (400,000 x 1.10) - (400,000 x 0.80) = 400,000 x 0.30 = £120,000

However, these costs do not consider potential changes in the Indian rupee versus British pound and additional costs from off-shoring (e.g., offshoring coordinator or partner in India, etc.).

Question 3: The CEO calls your team up for a quick update. What would you say to her?

Our initial findings show that we could potentially save substantial cost savings from offshoring due to lower labor costs, equipment costs, and raw materials' cost, but that would be partially offset by higher transportation or delivery costs.

However, aside from cost savings, we also need to consider potential revenue gains from starting an Asian offshoring location, as well as potentially risks such as the likelihood of lower quality of goods, etc.

We will need to conduct further investigation into these additional factors to get a more accurate analysis.

Question 4: The client has a base of loyal customers and wants to understand how offshoring might impact their customer behavior. The client shares that their current consumers are very sensitive about the quality of non-disposable goods, such as latex beds, and less sensitive about the quality for disposable goods, such as latex gloves. How might this information impact your team's recommendation?

Yes, as mentioned, cost savings are not sufficient to base a decision of whether to offshore. We would need to understand the impact of multiple other factors, of which, customer preference and behavior is an important one. The information that current consumers are very sensitive about the quality of certain goods will impact our team's recommendation depending on the size of the impact on the company's sales. We would need to size how the potential decline in quality would impact sales and how that compares to the potential cost savings.

Additionally, since consumers are very sensitive about the quality of non-disposable goods, such as latex beds, and less sensitive about the quality for disposable goods, such as latex gloves, even if this does not offset the cost savings, this could lead to a more diverse solution. For example, one potential strategy could be to offshore the production of disposable goods while keeping non-disposable goods produced at current plants. This could be a potential win-win option where we could capture some cost savings from the offshoring of non-disposable goods, but also keep and increase sales by maintaining consumer surplus.

Olympics Host

Problem statement

Your client is the city government of Madrid, which is considering a bid to host the next summer Olympic games. They have asked our team to help them decide if they should submit a bid.

Question 1: What are the key areas you would investigate to decide if the city should host the next Olympic games?

- Pros

- Additional revenue streams to the city:

    o TV rights

    o Ticket sales

    o Restaurant sales

    o Hotel occupancy

    o Souvenirs / merchandise sales

    o Transportation sales

    o More taxes collected (e.g., hotel occupancy, sales tax, etc.)

- Long-term benefits / changes to the city:

    o New businesses open in the city in anticipation of the Olympics

    o Improvements in infrastructure in

the city to host the Olympics

- ○ Prestige from hosting the Olympics

Cons / Risks

- Economic:

  - ○ Huge investments need to be poured into improving infrastructure to host the large crowds that the Olympics will bring. Examples of infrastructure could be roads, public transportation, sporting facilities, hotel venues, signage, cleaning facilities, gardening, and landscaping

- Socio / political:

  - ○ Additional traffic and congestion for the time period of the Olympic games

  - ○ Poorly hosted Olympic games would reflect very badly on the city

  - ○ Messy and negative impression to tourists if infrastructure improvements are not done well

- Security

  - ○ Potential risks of terrorism

  - ○ Potential security issues given large numbers of people streaming into the city during the Olympic games

Question 2: The team believes that the potential revenue gains could be very substantial. How would you go about sizing the potential revenue gains to

the city from ticket sales to the Olympic games?

We will apply a bottoms-up approach to sizing the ticket sales.

- Ticket sales = no. of tickets sold x price of each ticket

    o No. of tickets sold depend on the size of venue

    o Price of tickets differ depending on the stage of competition and other factors such as type of sport, etc.

- For no. of tickets sold, let us assume that there are three different venue sizes: small, medium, large

    o We can assume an approximate capacity for each venue, and therefore the corresponding number of tickets available for sale

    o Small: 1,000 seats

    o Medium: 10,000 seats

    o Large: 100,000 seats

- For price of tickets, let us assume that there are three main stages of competition, and for this sizing, we will assume that an average across all the 33 sports in the Olympic games

    o Initial Rounds: $50 average

    o Quarterfinals and Semifinals: $100 average

    o Finals: $500 average

- Assuming that all initial rounds are held in small venues, all quarterfinals and semifinals are held in medium venues, and all finals are held in large venues, we can calculate what the approximate ticket sales would be.

- Assuming 10 small venues, on average, required per initial round of a sport: Initial rounds across all sports = 33 x 10 x 1,000 x $50 = $16,500,000 or ~$16.5M

    o Assume 50% occupancy of venues = $16.5M x 50% = $8.25M

- Assuming 3 medium venues, on average, required per quarterfinals and semifinals round of a sport:

    o Quarterfinals and semifinals across all sports = 33 x 3 x 10,000 x $100 = $100M

    o Assume 70% occupancy of venues = $100M x 70% = $70M

- Assuming 1 large venue, on average, for finals of a sport:

    o Finals across all sports = 33 x 1 x 100,000 x $500 = $1.65B

    o Assume 80% occupancy of final venues = $1.65B x 80% = $1.32B

- Total estimated ticket sales = $8.25M + $70M + ~$1.32B = ~$1.4B

Question 3: From your findings, do you think the city of Madrid should host the next Olympic games?

Our initial findings show that the city of Madrid could stand to make a significant amount of revenue from ticket sales alone. The rest of Madrid will also benefit from increased tourism, etc.

However, we need to weigh the potential economic benefit of the Olympics against the investment needed by the city of Madrid in hosting the Olympics (e.g., infrastructure improvements), and also the potential risks from a socio political viewpoint and security perspective. The potential downsides of a terrorist attack, for example, are also enormous.

Additional research is needed to weigh and include these other factors in our cost-benefit analysis.

YOUR FUTURE AWAITS

C ongrats! You have done all of the practice cases and prepped your answers and stories for the behavioral fit portion of the interview. You are now ready to tackle your consulting interviews. You might read news articles about the incredibly low statistics of successful consulting candidates or hear horror stories from friends of how they completely bombed their interviews. Your imagination might start wandering off in all sorts of directions. Halt your thinking right there.

Thinking Positively

We have all been in scenarios where we imagine the worst. We mess up, we make a mistake, and we fail to achieve our goal. Yet thinking negatively is never helpful. Remember, this is all in your mind. Thinking negatively is like a rocking chair, it gives you something to do, but gets you nowhere.

Instead, imagine yourself succeeding. Imagine getting an invite to your first consulting interview. Imagine acing your interviews. Imagine that moment when the firm calls you to give you an offer. You have prepared long and hard for the interview process, and you need to believe in your own capabilities.

Pump Yourself Up

Before you head into your interviews, give yourself a little pep talk. People do this in many ways, whether it is just talking to themselves right before they go into the room, or whether it is looking into a mirror and giving themselves an encouraging speech or whether it is grabbing a friend to voice some encouragement to you on your interview days. Do whatever helps you to boost your energy, morale, and give you a fighting spirit in that interview room.

Get A Good Night's Sleep

Go to sleep at a reasonable time during the night before your interviews. Practice good sleeping habits in general, but especially the night before your interviews. You will likely perform better on a full night's sleep when you are feeling rested and energized. Put away your interview prep notes, meditate, or calm yourself down, and let your body relax. Stay away from blue-light emitting devices such as your computer or phone as that can keep you up and prevent you from feeling sleepy.

Have Fun

Armed with all these interview tools, go in there and have fun. Hopefully, you have enjoyed doing these practice case interviews and are excited about a career in consulting. If you are having fun, you will also likely perform better during your interviews because you would be relaxed, confident, and exude a passion for solving the case problem.

Case Closed!

CASE CLOSED

Made in the USA
Coppell, TX
12 July 2024

34560128R00113